CARDIOMETABOLIC RISK
IN CLINICAL PRACTICE

Dr Richard Clark
Dr Pam Brown
Dr Colin Kenny

Foreword by Professor Clifford J Bailey, Head of Diabetes, Aston University

Science Editor: Dr Scott Chambers
Production Editor: Emma Catherall
Operations Manager: Julia Savory
Designer: Jamie McCansh
Typesetter: Julie Smith
Publishing Director: Julian Grover
Publisher: Stephen I'Anson

The content of *Cardiometabolic Risk in Clinical Practice* has been produced in line with our standard editorial procedures. Whilst every effort has been made to ensure the accuracy of the information at the date of approval for publication, the Authors, the Publisher and the Editors accept no responsibility whatsoever for any errors or omissions or for any consequences arising from anything included in or excluded from *Cardiometabolic Risk in Clinical Practice*.

ISBN-10: 1-905466-42-0
ISBN-13: 978-190546-642-9

Typeset by Creative, Langbank, Scotland.
Printed and bound in Great Britain.

Contents

Foreword

Professor Cliff Bailey PhD, FRCP (Edin), FRCPath
Professor of Clinical Science, Aston University, Birmingham

From middle-age onwards almost everyone carries a portfolio of cardiovascular risk. For many this will translate into chronically debilitating atherothrombotic morbidity and premature mortality. Recognising and managing cardiovascular risk are now high priority – emphasised by governmental bodies, professional institutions and patient advocacy groups. Primary care stands at the sharp end of delivery, and this book describes how to meet the challenge.

Cardiometabolic risk is a variable composite of non-modifiable factors (such as ethnicity and family history) and a long list of modifiable factors. Foremost amongst the latter are central adiposity, raised blood pressure, dyslipidaemia, hyperglycaemia and hypercoagulability. These are frequently compounded by a sedentary lifestyle with inappropriate diet, smoking, excess alcohol and stress. The frequency with which cardiometabolic risk factors are prone to cluster within an individual has been embraced by the term 'metabolic syndrome'. This can provide a helpful basis for diagnosis, though the area has become clouded by the growing selection of differing definitions and interpretations. It is also important to take account of cardiovascular risks that are not included within the syndrome.

Insulin resistance, often associated with compensatory hyperinsulinaemia, is a common underlying disturbance in the development of cardiometabolic risk. Low-level inflammatory processes and oxidative stress also appear to contribute to the complex aetiology. This gives rise to considerable heterogeneity in both presentation and progression to cardiovascular disease, creating problems for diagnosis and the design of intervention strategies. To add to these burdens, the physician is now confronted with a minefield of guidelines, targets and contractual commitments. Moreover, multiple risk factors provide a recipe for multiple therapies which in turn can be costly, complicated and compromise compliance. Dealing with these conundrums is tugging ever harder at the resources of primary care: why not let this book take the strain?

Starting with a sound foundation in the pathogenesis of cardiometabolic risk, the authors examine the rationale for early and intensive management, looking particularly to minimise disease progression. Each section offers clear practical advice, showing the evidence base and its application in a primary care setting. Included here are the logistics of organising a local network, establishing registers and clinics, bringing together a multidisciplinary team, preparing individualised care plans, assessing and stratifying levels of risk, deciding which recommendations to follow, which targets to adopt and how to comply with National Service Framework (NSF) directives and the new General Medical Services (GMS) contract.

How to investigate who is at risk, and why? How to assess what that level of risk means for the individual? How and when should intervention be initiated, monitored and maintained? How and where do algorithms, guidelines and responsibilities fit in? 'How' is often the most difficult problem (a small word with a big connotation). This book is the 'how' for primary care. Its practical perspective will facilitate an informed and pragmatic approach to address cardiometabolic risk with confidence and reassurance. Your practice and your patients will benefit.

1. Overview of cardiometabolic disease

Introduction

Certain cardiovascular and metabolic disorders have a tendency to cluster together, predisposing individuals to an increased risk of cardiovascular disease (CVD)[a] and type 2 diabetes. These so-called cardiometabolic risk factors include insulin resistance or glucose intolerance, hypertension, dyslipidaemia and obesity (particularly central obesity). This cluster of disorders has historically been described as the metabolic syndrome. However, the exact definition of the metabolic syndrome, the relative importance of its constituent conditions and even its existence remain a subject of fierce debate (Box 1).[1–4]

> **Box 1.** Does the metabolic syndrome exist and, if so, is it a useful categorisation? A discussion following some of the queries advanced by the American Diabetes Association (ADA) and the European Association for the Study of Diabetes (EASD), and subsequent answers from the International Diabetes Federation (IDF).[1–4]
>
> **Question:** Is the metabolic syndrome a syndrome at all, as its precise cause is unknown?
>
> **Answer:** The clustering of risk factors for cardiovascular disease (CVD) and type 2 diabetes is a good basis for calling this a syndrome. In addition, there are other historical examples of syndromes such as type 2 diabetes where the underlying cause was not known.
>
> **Question:** Does the label 'the metabolic syndrome' serve a useful purpose?
>
> **Answer:** It serves a useful purpose by identifying individuals who are likely to develop CVD and/or type 2 diabetes and who are therefore at a substantial risk of significant morbidity and premature mortality. However, the exact cause of the metabolic syndrome is still unknown. Some have suggested a pivotal role for insulin resistance, others for central obesity. It seems likely that more than one factor is involved.
>
> **Question:** Is it just an exercise in 'labelling' driven by the pharmaceutical industry, and therefore 'medicalising' people unnecessarily?
>
> **Answer:** The concept of clustering of cardiovascular risk factors was first described in the 1920s when Kylin highlighted the association of hypertension, hyperglycaemia and gout.[1] Such clustering did not receive further attention until 1988, when Reaven first described syndrome X (insulin resistance, hyperglycaemia, hypertension, low levels of high density lipoprotein cholesterol [HDL-C] and high levels of very low density lipoprotein cholesterol [VLDL-C] and triglycerides).[2] Although he omitted obesity – which is considered by many as the essential component of the metabolic syndrome – the essence of syndrome X is now most commonly described as the metabolic syndrome.

[a]For the purpose of this book, cardiovascular disease comprises coronary heart disease (CHD), stroke and transient ischaemic attack (TIA).

Regardless of the detail of the debate, from a practical perspective it is apparent that a greater understanding of cardiometabolic risk amongst healthcare professionals will raise awareness that:

- risk factors for CVD and diabetes cluster together and act in concert to amplify the risk of developing these diseases
- identification of one risk factor in any one individual should prompt a search for other risk factors
- there is a need to treat all risk factors that cluster together in order to reduce the total risk of CVD and diabetes.

Interesting times lie ahead in the field of chronic disease management in general and the management of cardiometabolic disease in particular. The UK is facing an increasing prevalence of coronary heart disease (CHD), diabetes, hypertension, dyslipidaemia and obesity. Healthcare professionals, particularly those working at the forefront of disease management in primary care, need to adopt new and efficient methods of working to manage this constellation of diseases as effectively as possible. However, the clustering of cardiometabolic risk factors within individuals can work to our advantage on a practical level. By managing these risk factors together as a single entity (i.e. as cardiometabolic disease) rather than as separate diseases, we can optimise patient care and maximise limited healthcare resources.

Throughout this book, we will offer practical advice on how healthcare workers can set about managing cardiometabolic risk factors and highlight the benefits that such an approach can yield in terms of saving practice time and avoiding duplicate consultations for multiple risk factor intervention.

By managing risk factors together as a single entity (i.e. as cardiometabolic disease), we can optimise patient care and maximise limited healthcare resources.

Background to cardiometabolic disease

The concept of cardiometabolic disease was formulated to link the disorders of the metabolic syndrome to CVD and type 2 diabetes, for which they are known to be predictive factors.[5]

For example:

- obesity (particularly central obesity) is a predisposing factor for the development of type 2 diabetes, hypertension and CVD
- obesity and type 2 diabetes are intimately associated with insulin resistance
- central obesity is linked with hyperinsulinaemia, insulin resistance, dyslipidaemia and proinflammatory and prothrombotic clinical states.[6]

Physical inactivity, poor diet, ageing and genetic factors appear to be underlying factors that link the metabolic syndrome to CVD and type 2 diabetes (Figure 1).[5]

If metabolic and cardiovascular diseases are viewed as a continuum, then these disorders individually and interdependently increase the risk of morbidity and mortality from CVD. On the other hand, an understanding of the inter-related nature of these disorders and influencing risk factors provides clinicians with practical opportunities for lifestyle and therapeutic

An understanding of the inter-related nature of these disorders and influencing risk factors provides clinicians with practical opportunities to improve cardiometabolic health.

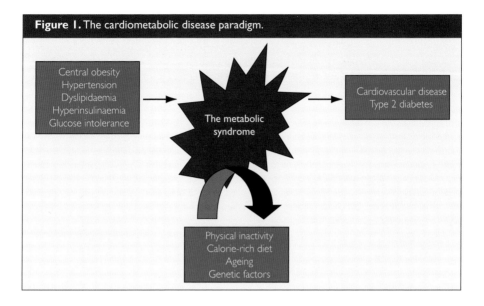

Figure 1. The cardiometabolic disease paradigm.

Central obesity
Hypertension
Dyslipidaemia
Hyperinsulinaemia
Glucose intolerance

The metabolic syndrome

Cardiovascular disease
Type 2 diabetes

Physical inactivity
Calorie-rich diet
Ageing
Genetic factors

interventions to improve cardiometabolic health. Improved diet, increased physical activity and better control of blood pressure, dyslipidaemia and glycaemia all have beneficial effects on CVD morbidity and mortality.[5] By identifying patient populations at high cardiometabolic risk and intervening appropriately, we can prevent progression to type 2 diabetes and minimise future cardiovascular events.[7] This strategy is referred to as primary prevention. The recent publication of the second Joint British Societies (JBS 2) guidelines on prevention of CVD in clinical practice places an equal focus on primary prevention in high-risk individuals and secondary prevention in those with established CVD and diabetes.[8]

In this chapter we will investigate the latest scientific thinking relating to cardiometabolic risk and will cover key concepts such as:

- diagnosis of the metabolic syndrome and its components
- epidemiology of the metabolic syndrome and its components
- risk factors and aetiology
- pathophysiology of cardiometabolic disease
- clinical guidelines and clinical management.

Diagnosis

It is more common to consider the diagnosis of the metabolic syndrome or its individual component conditions rather than cardiometabolic disease *per se*. Confusingly, several different diagnostic criteria for the metabolic syndrome are in usage (Boxes 2 and 3).[3,9–11] Whilst these definitions share many features, each varies slightly according to certain aspects of the syndrome (e.g. glycaemia or central obesity).

Box 2. Definitions of the metabolic syndrome from the World Health Organization (WHO), the European Group for the Study of Insulin Resistance (EGIR) and the National Cholesterol Education Program (NCEP).[9–11] (Adapted from the British Nutrition Foundation; *www.nutrition.org.uk*)

WHO 1999[10]
Diabetes or impaired glucose tolerance or insulin resistance plus **two** of the following.
- Dyslipidaemia:
  – triglycerides >1.7 mmol/L; HDL-C <0.9 mmol/L (men) and <1.0 mmol/L (females)
- Hypertension:
  – blood pressure >140/90 mmHg and/or medication
- Obesity:
  – BMI >30 and/or WHR >0.9 (males) or >0.85 (females)
- Microalbuminuria

EGIR 1999[11]
Insulin resistance or hyperinsulinaemia (non-diabetics only) plus **two** of the following.
- Fasting plasma glucose >6.1 mmol/L
- Dyslipidaemia:
  – triglycerides >2.0 mmol/L and/or HDL-C <1.0 mmol/L or treated for dyslipidaemia
- Hypertension:
  – blood pressure >140/90 mmHg and/or medication
- Central obesity:
  – waist circumference >94 cm (males), >80 cm (females)

NCEP 2001[9]
Three of the following.
- Fasting plasma glucose >6.1 mmol/L
- Hypertriglyceridaemia
  – triglycerides >1.7 mmol/L
- Low HDL-C
- Hypertension:
  – blood pressure >130/85 mmHg and/or medication
- Central obesity:
  – waist circumference >102 cm (males), >88 cm (females)

Recently, the International Diabetes Federation (IDF) attempted to resolve some of the problems surrounding the issues of cardiometabolic disease and the metabolic syndrome by publishing a new definition (see Box 3).[3] This aimed to:
- end the confusion surrounding the multiple diagnostic criteria in current usage
- identify individuals at high risk of CVD and diabetes
- be applicable to different ethnic groups
- allow for comparative long-term studies to further refine the definition.

Box 3. International Diabetes Federation (IDF) definition of the metabolic syndrome.[3]

Central obesity
Waist circumference above ethnicity specific cut points[a] (Box 4)

Plus any two from:

Raised triglycerides
>1.7 mmol/L OR
On treatment for this lipid abnormality

Reduced high density lipoprotein cholesterol (HDL-C)
<1.03 mmol/L in men
<1.29 mmol/L in women OR
On treatment for this lipid abnormality

Raised blood pressure
Systolic blood pressure ≥130 mmHg
Diastolic blood pressure ≥85 mmHg OR
Treatment of previously diagnosed hypertension

Raised fasting plasma glucose[b]
Fasting plasma glucose ≥5.6 mmol/L
Previously diagnosed type 2 diabetes
If above 5.6 mmol/L, an oral glucose tolerance test is strongly recommended, but is not necessary to define the presence of the metabolic syndrome.

[a]If body mass index (BMI) is over 30 kg/m², central obesity can be assumed and waist circumference does not need to be measured.
[b]In clinical practice, impaired glucose tolerance (IGT) is also acceptable, but all reports of prevalence of metabolic syndrome should use only fasting plasma glucose and presence of previously diagnosed diabetes to define hyperglycaemia. Prevalences also incorporating 2-hour glucose results can be added as supplementary findings.

The IDF argued that diabetes and insulin resistance were overemphasised in early criteria and instead built upon the less 'glucocentric' criteria of the US National Cholesterol Education Program (NCEP) Adult Treatment Panel III (ATP III) for its definition. The main change placed central obesity **(assessed by waist circumference)** as **the** core measurement. This was for two underlying reasons.

- The strength of evidence linking waist circumference with CVD and other components of the metabolic syndrome.
- The likelihood that central obesity is an early step in the pathological processes leading to the metabolic syndrome.

Ethnic-specific waist circumference cut-off points were also incorporated into the IDF definition, further increasing its practical utility (Box 4).

Recently, the INTERHEART study – a landmark case-controlled study conducted in more than 50 countries – identified nine risk factors (smoking, hypertension, diabetes, abdominal obesity, diet, physical activity, alcohol, lipid profile and psychosocial factors) which accounted

Box 4. International Diabetes Federation (IDF) definition of the metabolic syndrome: ethnic-specific values for waist circumference.[3] Data are pragmatic cut-offs and better data are required to link them to risk.

Ethnic group[a]	Waist circumference (as a measure of central obesity)
Europids	
Men	≥94 cm
Women	≥80 cm
South Asians	
Men	≥90 cm
Women	≥80 cm
Chinese	
Men	≥90 cm
Women	≥80 cm
Japanese	
Men	≥85 cm
Women	≥90 cm
Ethnic South and Central Americans	Use South Asian recommendations until more specific data are available
Sub-Saharan Africans	Use European recommendations until more specific data are available
Eastern Mediterranean and Middle East (Arab) populations	Use European recommendations until more specific data are available

Ethnicity and not country of residence should be the basis for classification.

[a]In the USA, National Cholesterol Education Program Adult Treatment Panel III (NCEP ATP III) values (i.e. ≥102 cm for males and ≥88 cm for females) are still likely to be used for clinical purposes. In future epidemiological studies in Europid populations (i.e. Caucasians of European origin, regardless of where they live in the world), prevalence should be given with both European and North American cut-offs to allow better comparisons of these data.

for virtually all of the risk for an initial acute myocardial infarction (MI) in a broad and ethnically diverse population.[12] Abdominal obesity, in this case determined by the **waist-to-hip ratio,** was shown to be a better predictor of risk than other measurements of obesity, including BMI.[13]

Establishing a unified definition of the metabolic syndrome will form the basis for further research into this area using standardised criteria and will allow for comparisons between different studies conducted in different countries. The IDF also identified certain criteria for further research, which will allow for a refined definition in the future based on

Establishing a unified definition of the metabolic syndrome will form the basis for further research into this area using standardised criteria.

the predictive power of these additional risk factors for CVD and diabetes. Examples of these additional cardiometabolic criteria include:

- abnormal body fat distribution (e.g. by magnetic resonance imaging [MRI])
- dyslipidaemia (e.g. small, dense low density lipoprotein [LDL] particles)
- vascular dysregulation (e.g. endothelial dysfunction, microalbuminuria)
- proinflammatory and prothrombotic states.

Epidemiology

There are few data available regarding the epidemiology of the metabolic syndrome *per se*. Given the confusion generated from having different definitions of the syndrome, it is very difficult to generalise about the prevalence of the metabolic syndrome in a community setting. However, if we put the debate about these definitions to one side, we can obtain a rough idea of the prevalence of the syndrome from several published studies (Table 1).[14–17]

Some of the strongest data concerning the epidemiology of the metabolic syndrome come from the US National Health and Nutrition Examination Survey (NHANES).[14] This survey reported an age-adjusted prevalence of 24% amongst more than 20,000 adults. The prevalence of the syndrome increased with age – from 7% in the 20–29-year age group to 44% in those aged 60–69 years.[14] Moreover, the prevalence of the metabolic syndrome has continued to increase over time, from an estimated 50 million in 1990 to 64 million in 2000 in the USA alone.[15] This increase is partly due to shifting demographics but there is a also 'real' increase in prevalence, primarily due to increases in waist circumference, hypertension and hypertriglyceridaemia.[15] As an illustration, in the USA between 1988 and 2000, waist circumference increased from an average of 96.0 to 98.6 cm for men and from 88.7 to 92.2 cm for women.[18]

In the following sections of this chapter, we will examine trends in prevalence of some of the main components of the metabolic syndrome and cardiometabolic disease. A particular emphasis will be placed on abdominal obesity as this appears to be a central feature within the

> The prevalence of the metabolic syndrome has continued to increase, from an estimated 50 million in 1990 to 64 million in 2000 in the USA alone.

Table 1. The prevalence of the metabolic syndrome.[14–17]		
Study	Population	Prevalence
Ford et al., 2002[14]	US men and women	24%
Ford et al., 2004[15]	US men and women	27%
Lakka et al., 2002[16]	Finnish men without a history of CVD or diabetes	14%
Lawlor et al., 2004[17]	UK women aged 60–79 years	28–29%

constellation of disorders comprising the metabolic syndrome, as recognised by the IDF.[3] This may help to establish a more accurate picture of the overall problem facing clinicians in the UK today.

Trends in epidemiology

Diabetes and impaired glucose metabolism

In recent years, there has been a huge increase in the number of cases of diabetes to such an extent that the situation is often described as a 'global pandemic'. The number of people with diabetes is predicted to rise from about 151 million in 2000 to more than 300 million by 2025 (Figure 2).[19–22] Most cases are type 2 diabetes, which has its highest prevalence in developed countries as it is strongly associated with obesity and sedentary lifestyles.[23]

In the UK:

- more than 2 million people are diagnosed with diabetes (equivalent to 3 in 100 people) but an estimated 1 million cases remain undiagnosed
- approximately 85–90% of all diabetics have type 2 disease.[19,24,25]

The prevalence of diabetes increases with age. In the UK, 1 in 20 people over the age of 65 and 1 in 5 over the age of 85 have type 2 diabetes.[25] However, these are probably conservative estimates as the impact of rises in obesity has not yet been fully accounted for.[22] Thus, we can expect further increases in the incidence of type 2 diabetes if the combined and related problems of obesity and inactivity are not tackled.

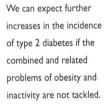

We can expect further increases in the incidence of type 2 diabetes if the combined and related problems of obesity and inactivity are not tackled.

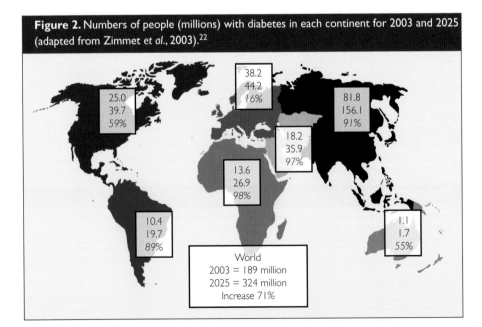

Figure 2. Numbers of people (millions) with diabetes in each continent for 2003 and 2025 (adapted from Zimmet *et al.*, 2003).[22]

38.2
44.2
16%

81.8
156.1
91%

25.0
39.7
59%

18.2
35.9
97%

13.6
26.9
98%

10.4
19.7
89%

1.1
1.7
55%

World
2003 = 189 million
2025 = 324 million
Increase 71%

It is important to realise that many people with cardiometabolic disease may not have progressed to type 2 diabetes but may have impaired glucose regulation, such as impaired glucose tolerance (IGT). Appropriate intervention in people with IGT – whether with diet, exercise and/or pharmacotherapy – can substantially reduce the risk of progression to type 2 diabetes.[22] Likewise, impaired fasting glycaemia (IFG) – another category of abnormal glucose metabolism – is also associated with an increased risk of type 2 diabetes. Like patients with diabetes, those with IGT or IFG are at greater risk of CVD than the general population.[22]

Obesity

Obesity has reached epidemic proportions and the number of people affected continues to increase.[18] Worldwide more than 1 billion adults are overweight and at least 300 million are classified as clinically obese.[26] The increase in obesity is particularly marked in the USA, where the largest increases in waist circumference occurred in the 20–29-year age group.[18] Over the past 30 years, the increase in obesity has paralleled the dramatic rise in the prevalence of diabetes.[27,28] The primary reason for the increase in obesity appears to be the spread of the Western lifestyle, characterised by energy-dense diets and physical inactivity.[29] Between 1967–69 and 1997–99, the intake of fat increased by approximately 31% across the countries of the European Community.[30] However, many believe that the problem of rising obesity relates primarily to decreased levels of physical activity rather than increased food intake *per se*. This is illustrated by the observation that whilst the prevalence of obesity in the UK increased by more than 150% between 1980 and 1997, food intake per household actually fell by 20%.[5,31]

Whatever the underlying reason for its increased prevalence, it is increasingly apparent that obesity is rapidly becoming the 'norm' in many Western societies. This will have a profound effect on future public health as excess weight, primarily when carried around the abdomen, is associated with an increased risk for a wide range of chronic conditions. These include type 2 diabetes, hypertension, dyslipidaemia, osteoarthritis, sleep apnoea, gallbladder disease, infertility and some cancers.[32] Abdominal obesity has also emerged as a direct cardiovascular risk factor (Box 5).[6]

On the basis of current trends, it has been estimated that one-quarter of all adults in England will be obese by 2010 (Figure 3).[34] However, obesity is preventable, and even modest reductions in weight can markedly reduce patients' exposure to the risk of morbidity and premature mortality. For example, it has been estimated that a loss of 10 kg can result in a 20–25% reduction in premature mortality.[32]

Box 6 summarises the terminology widely employed in the literature to describe the different types of body fat.[33]

Worldwide more than 1 billion adults are overweight and at least 300 million are classified as clinically obese.

Obesity is preventable, and even modest reductions in weight can markedly reduce patients' exposure to the risk of morbidity and premature mortality.

Box 5. Cardiovascular risk factors associated with abdominal obesity.[6]

- Insulin resistance/hyperinsulinaemia
- Hyperglycaemia
- Low concentrations of high density lipoprotein cholesterol (HDL-C)
- High triglyceride concentrations
- Increased apolipoprotein B concentrations
- Small, dense low density lipoprotein (LDL) particles
- Increased fibrinogen concentrations
- Increased production of plasminogen activator inhibitor (PAI)
- Increased concentrations of C-reactive protein (CRP)
- Increased production of tumour necrosis factor (TNF)
- Increased production of interleukin (IL)-6
- Microalbuminuria
- Increased blood viscosity
- Increased systolic blood pressure and pulse pressure
- Left ventricular hypertrophy
- Premature atherosclerosis
- Microalbuminuria

Hypertension

Hypertension affects 600 million people worldwide and results in the deaths of 3 million people every year.[35] In the USA, more than one-quarter of the population (about 50 million people) have hypertension.[36,37] The prevalence of hypertension in the UK is reported to be even higher, with 37% of adults aged over 16 years identified as being hypertensive.[38] These survey data differ from the incidence of hypertension reported in England from 52,833,584 registered patients across 8,486 practices, which estimated a national prevalence rate of just 11.3%.[39]

The prevalence of hypertension increases markedly with advancing age.[40,41] In the British Women's Heart and Health Study survey of 4,286 women aged 60–79 years, 50% were found to be hypertensive.[42] Thus, the prevalence of hypertension will increase in future years as the UK's population ages.

Persistently elevated blood pressure can have profound consequences for the individual as it:

- contributes to end-organ damage in the heart, brain, eyes and kidneys
- is a major risk factor for the development of CHD and underlying atherosclerosis
- increases the risk of stroke.[41,43,44]

The prevalence of hypertension will increase in future years as the UK's population ages.

Box 6. A summary of 'fat' terminology. Adapted from National Obesity Forum.[33]

Different types of fat confer different levels of risk

The location of excess fat makes a significant difference in terms of the cardiometabolic risk of the individual.

There are two principal stores of fat in the body:

- **subcutaneous fat**
- **intra-abdominal fat**

Subcutaneous fat is stored just below the skin relatively near to the surface of the body. It is a major determinant of serum leptin levels.

Intra-abdominal fat or visceral fat is stored around the major organs in the abdominal cavity. It plays a critical role in determining insulin sensitivity and an atherogenic lipid profile.

Intra-abdominal (visceral) fat is the most dangerous type fat in terms of cardiometabolic risk.

An excess of intra-abdominal fat leads to **central** or **visceral obesity**, defined as an excessive accumulation of fat cells around the major organs deep in the abdomen.

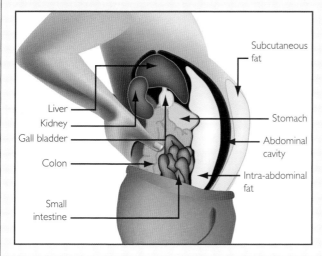

Hypertension remains a major public health problem and is one of the leading causes of death and disability worldwide after smoking and malnutrition, and is also a major independent risk factor for CVD.[45] Although substantial progress has been made in the diagnosis and treatment of the condition in recent years, blood pressure is normalised in less than one-third of treated hypertensive patients, leading to serious long-term health problems for the individuals concerned, to say nothing

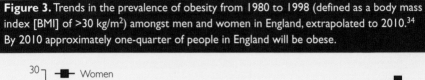

Figure 3. Trends in the prevalence of obesity from 1980 to 1998 (defined as a body mass index [BMI] of >30 kg/m^2) amongst men and women in England, extrapolated to 2010.[34] By 2010 approximately one-quarter of people in England will be obese.

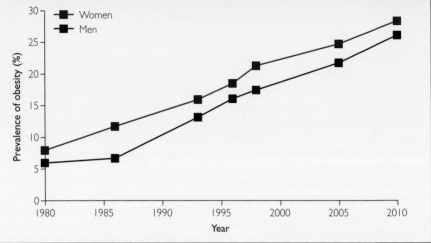

of the millions of hypertensives who remain undiagnosed.[46] Furthermore, as hypertension is known to be associated with obesity, its prevalence will continue to increase as the epidemic of obesity in the developed world takes hold.[47]

Dyslipidaemia

The term 'lipid lowering' is often used when describing the management of dyslipidaemia. However, this can be misleading. Patients with poor glycaemic control (such as those with type 2 diabetes) typically have a dyslipidaemia characterised by high triglycerides and reduced levels of cardioprotective high density lipoprotein cholesterol (HDL-C).[48] Levels of total cholesterol and LDL-C are often normal in patients with type 2 diabetes, particularly if glycaemic control is adequate.[49] In contrast, patients with poor glycaemic control often have a qualitative abnormality in their LDL-C fraction, characterised by a preponderance of small, dense and highly atherogenic LDL particles.[48,50] This pattern of lipid abnormality, characterised by small dense LDL-C, elevated triglycerides and low HDL-C, is commonly referred to as the atherogenic lipid triad or atherogenic dyslipidaemia (Figure 4) and is characteristic of both the metabolic syndrome and type 2 diabetes.[51,52] Indeed, hypertriglyceridaemia and low HDL-C contribute to the IDF definition of the metabolic syndrome. Unfortunately, primary care cannot usually obtain subgroup analyses of LDL particles and, therefore, this type of dyslipidaemia can only be

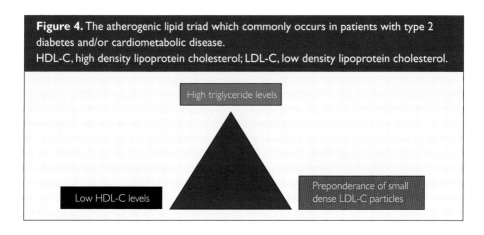

Figure 4. The atherogenic lipid triad which commonly occurs in patients with type 2 diabetes and/or cardiometabolic disease.
HDL-C, high density lipoprotein cholesterol; LDL-C, low density lipoprotein cholesterol.

predicted on the basis of other elements of the lipid profiles and the clinical history of the patient.

There is a distinct lack of epidemiological data regarding the prevalence of the atherogenic dyslipidaemia typical of cardiometabolic disease. However, it is becoming increasingly apparent that hypertriglyceridaemia, in addition to high LDL-C and total cholesterol levels, is a strong predictor of CHD. High triglyceride levels ($\geq$2.3 mmol/L) are associated with a doubling in the risk of CHD mortality or morbidity, independently of other risk factors.[53] Furthermore, low levels of HDL-C appear to be an independent risk factor for CVD.[54] Likewise, small, dense LDL-C particles are highly atherogenic as they are more likely to form oxidised LDL, and are also less readily cleared from the circulation.[49,51] The atherogenic lipid triad has been proposed as the major driving force for coronary atherosclerosis, and is predictive of cardiovascular events in patients with type 2 diabetes.[55]

> The atherogenic lipid triad has been proposed as the major driving force for coronary atherosclerosis, and is predictive of cardiovascular events in patients with type 2 diabetes.

CVD risk factors and aetiology

In the previous section we considered the epidemiology and the CVD risks surrounding the individual components of the metabolic syndrome. Here, we will briefly review the risk posed by cardiometabolic disease, as well as modifiable lifestyle risk factors and genetic (unmodifiable) risks.

Metabolic syndrome

Patients with the metabolic syndrome are reported to have an approximate five-fold increased risk of type 2 diabetes and a two-to-three-fold increased risk of CVD.[56] The impact of the metabolic syndrome on the risk of CVD and diabetes has been assessed in several large-scale studies.

- A 13-year follow-up of 6,255 individuals showed that the metabolic syndrome strongly predicted the development of CVD and was

The metabolic syndrome
predicted CVD and total
mortality more strongly
than the individual
components that
comprise the syndrome.

associated with increased total mortality.[57] Even individuals with only one or two risk factors for the metabolic syndrome were at an increased risk of future mortality from CVD. Moreover, the metabolic syndrome predicted CVD and total mortality more strongly than did the individual components that comprise the syndrome.

- A study of 1,209 Finnish men with the metabolic syndrome demonstrated that the syndrome is a risk factor for CHD and premature cardiovascular mortality and morbidity.[16] Patients were between two- and three-times more likely to have CVD or to die from CHD.
- Individuals with the metabolic syndrome in the NHANES survey were at an increased risk of MI (odds ratio [OR] 2.0), stroke (OR 2.1) and either MI or stroke (OR 2.0), compared with those without the syndrome.[58] The metabolic syndrome was also significantly associated with either MI or stroke in both men and women in this survey.

Modifiable risk factors

Modifiable cardiometabolic risk factors include sedentary lifestyle and poor diet, though the impact of these factors may be influenced via a heightened risk of obesity and the concomitant risks associated with the obese state.

Smoking is another modifiable risk factor for the development of CVD. Increasing the numbers of cigarettes smoked increases premature mortality in a linear fashion.[59] This risk is increased according to:

- the number of cigarettes smoked
- the extent of inhalation
- the age when smoking began
- the number of years spent smoking
- the tar yield of the preferred cigarette.[59,60]

Non-modifiable risk factors

CVD has a tendency to
cluster in families, so it is
essential that clinicians
always take a family
history when determining
an individual's level of risk.

Non-modifiable risk factors include hereditary risk factors (e.g. a family history of CVD and/or diabetes) and comorbid disease (e.g. secondary hypertension). However, these aspects lie beyond the scope of this book. It is probably more important to emphasise that CVD has a tendency to cluster in families, so it is essential that clinicians always take a family history when determining an individual's level of risk.[8]

Pathophysiology

The association of obesity (in particular intra-abdominal or central obesity) with the various components of the metabolic syndrome appears to be driven by the biology of adipose tissue. Although BMI can be used as a crude diagnostic marker to screen for overweight and obesity, only waist circumference or the waist-to-hip ratio can be used to diagnose central obesity (Box 7). [8,13,60,61] As we have seen, amongst the overweight

Box 7. Central obesity – the importance of measuring waist circumference.[8,13,60,61]

- The body mass index (BMI) provides a simple and convenient measurement of obesity. However, evidence shows that weight gain alone is not the only problem. Rather, it is the regional distribution of excess body fat that is more important than obesity *per se* in predicting cardiovascular risk and thus cardiovascular mortality and morbidity.

- Central obesity is common in men, whose 'pot bellies' make them appear 'apple shaped'. In contrast, women frequently tend to be 'pear shaped', with excess fat located around the hips and buttocks.[60]

- The importance of abdominal obesity is particularly apparent in Asian populations, which tend to have high levels of intra-abdominal fat even at low BMIs, making these individuals particularly prone to type 2 diabetes, hypertension and coronary heart disease.[60]

- The waist-to-hip ratio was previously thought of as a less reliable measure of central obesity, particularly if fat deposition occurred equally around the hips and waist, as the ratio remains unchanged.

- However, INTERHEART demonstrated that abdominal obesity – as measured by waist-to-hip ratio (WHR; high WHR defined as >0.83 in women and >0.9 in men) – was an independent risk factor for acute myocardial infarction and was also a stronger predictor of such events than BMI and waist circumference alone.[13] The authors of this landmark study suggested that such measurements of abdominal obesity should replace BMI as an indicator of obesity and thus cardiovascular risk.[13]

- Waist circumference is acknowledged to be the best simple measurement of central obesity as shown by its correlation with computed tomography (CT) scanning.[61] Moreover, it is the most convenient and straightforward measurement of central obesity in practice. The recent JBS 2 guidelines also argue that measurement of waist circumference is the most practical method of determining abdominal obesity in clinical practice.[8]

and obese, it is those individuals with abdominal obesity who are at the greatest risk of developing CVD.

The Paris Prospective Study showed that increases in central obesity were paralleled by an increased risk of sudden death.[62] Furthermore, central obesity (measured by waist circumference or waist-to-hip ratio) is a key predictor of metabolic and cardiovascular risk and is a more accurate marker than the measurement of BMI alone.[13,62,63]

Central obesity has emerged as an important cardiovascular risk factor in its own right.[63] Although the processes leading to this increased cardiovascular risk are not fully understood, central obesity is associated with a range of established CVD risk factors (e.g. insulin resistance, atherogenic dyslipidaemia and hypertension) plus other factors such as increased coagulability, endothelial dysfunction and inflammation.[6]

The role of adipose tissue

Historically, adipose tissue was considered to be a passive depot for the storage of excess calories. More recently, however, it has been shown that

Metabolically active cells
in adipose tissue (the
adipocytes) secrete
biologically active
molecules that can
influence other
CVD risk factors.

metabolically active cells in adipose tissue (the adipocytes) secrete biologically active molecules that can influence other CVD risk factors. In simple terms, in the pathological state of excess intra-abdominal adiposity, the higher volume and activity of metabolically active visceral fat cells leads to enhanced synthesis of these bioactive molecules, in turn contributing to a heightened cardiovascular risk.

The primary function of adipocytes is the storage and release of energy. During the fasting state, adipocytes break down triglycerides (via lipolysis) to make energy available for use (e.g. as fatty acids). However, in the postprandial state the balance shifts back towards lipogenesis (i.e. the process of storing energy as triglycerides). Adipocytes also produce various chemical messengers, which appear to increase CVD risk in patients with central obesity. These include proinflammatory cytokines, such as interleukin (IL)-6, tumour necrosis factor (TNF)-α and plasminogen activator inhibitor (PAI)-1, vasoactive substances and other peptides known as adipokines (e.g. adiponectin).[6] The role of these inflammatory mediators and substances in patients with central obesity is considered in more detail in Box 8.[6,64] The network of atherogenic factors associated with central obesity and possible mechanisms by which they contribute to cardiometabolic disease are illustrated in Figure 5.

Box 8. Biologically active molecules secreted by adipocytes which influence cardiovascular risk in patients with central obesity.[6,64]

Adiponectin

Lower levels of adiponectin are associated with central obesity. This molecule has three main effects:

- increased hepatic insulin resistance (decreased effect of insulin in inhibiting hepatic glucose production)
- decreased high density lipoprotein cholesterol (HDL-C) and a preponderance of small, dense low density lipoprotein (LDL) particles
- impaired insulin action in peripheral tissues, resulting in a less efficient glucose uptake and deposition of triglyceride in the muscles.

Tumour necrosis factor (TNF)-α and interleukin (IL)-6

The proinflammatory cytokine, TNF-α, is produced by adipose tissue. TNF-α regulates the acute-phase protein, C-reactive protein (CRP), via the production of IL-6.

- Overexpression of TNF-α occurs in the adipocytes of obese individuals, and this induces IL-6, a prime regulator of the acute-phase response.
- This can lead to a characteristically proinflammatory state in obese individuals which contributes to the overall risk for acute coronary events.

Plasminogen activator inhibitor (PAI)-1

PAI-1 is an inhibitor of fibrinolysis and it is found in higher concentrations in obese individuals.

- The total amount of visceral adipose tissue correlates with PAI-1 activity.
- Increased PAI-1 levels contribute to the prothrombotic state which may promote atherogenesis and increases the risk of CVD.

Figure 5. The network of atherogenic factors associated with central obesity and possible mechanisms by which they contribute to cardiometabolic disease.[6]
CRP, C-reactive protein; HDL-C, high density lipoprotein cholesterol; IL-6, interleukin-6; LDL, low density lipoprotein; PAI-1, plasminogen activator inhibitor-1; TNF-α, tumour necrosis factor-α.

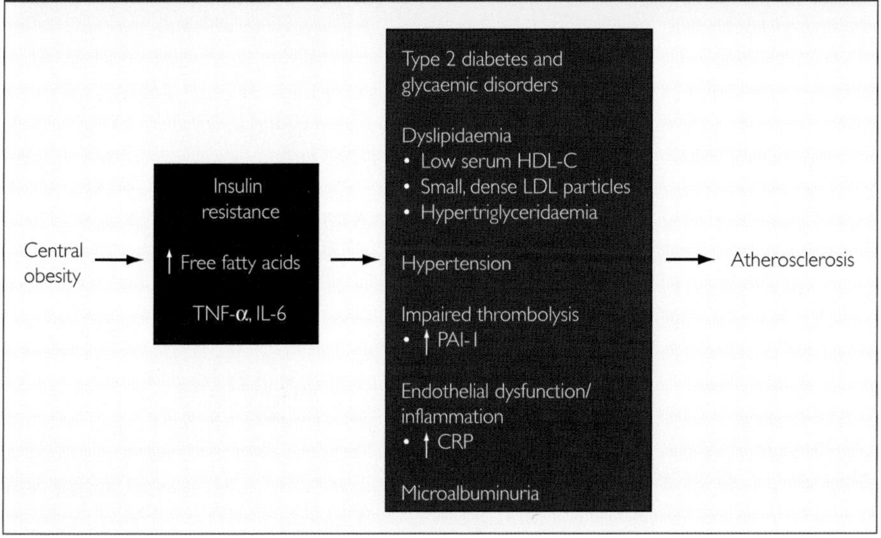

```
Central
obesity  →  Insulin
            resistance

            ↑ Free fatty acids

            TNF-α, IL-6   →   Type 2 diabetes and
                              glycaemic disorders

                              Dyslipidaemia
                              • Low serum HDL-C
                              • Small, dense LDL particles
                              • Hypertriglyceridaemia

                              Hypertension          →   Atherosclerosis

                              Impaired thrombolysis
                              • ↑ PAI-1

                              Endothelial dysfunction/
                              inflammation
                              • ↑ CRP

                              Microalbuminuria
```

Reducing cardiometabolic risk

Managing cardiometabolic risk requires an aggressive approach, with a combined focus on lifestyle modification and pharmacological intervention. Recommendations for lifestyle change should be given to patients with central obesity, with advice focused on increasing physical activity and improving diet. In overweight and obese patients, weight loss is associated with decreases in central obesity and this can improve insulin sensitivity and reduce risk factors for CVD, such as hypertension, serum triglycerides, HDL-C and small, dense LDL particles.[6] Furthermore, there is increasing evidence that exercise-induced weight loss in individuals with central obesity promotes a faster rate of loss of visceral fat than whole body fat, which may thereby further reduce cardiovascular risk.[65]

Many pharmacological interventions are available to correct hypertension, dyslipidaemia, hyperglycaemia and obesity. These strategies will be discussed in more detail in the following chapter of this book. Recently, there has been growing interest in combination therapy in order to maximise treatment outcomes, including the concept of the 'polypill'.[66] It has been suggested that all people with pre-existing CVD (i.e. a secondary prevention population) and, more controversially, all adults aged over 55 years (i.e. a primary prevention population) would benefit from a polypill.[66] The polypill should comprise six individual

Managing cardiometabolic disease requires an aggressive approach, with a combined focus on lifestyle modification and pharmacological intervention.

components at lower than standard doses: a thiazide diuretic, an angiotensin-converting enzyme (ACE) inhibitor, a β-blocker, a statin, aspirin and folic acid. Clinical evidence is still required to test this hypothesis, though recent data from a large number of UK patients seem to confirm that combinations of statins, aspirin and β-blockers (but not an ACE inhibitor) improved survival in high-risk patients with CVD.[67] We are still a long way away from firm clinical evidence for the polypill, though the concept seems to be a reasonable one, at least for secondary prevention.

Another recent innovation has been the introduction of novel agents such as rimonabant. This drug targets the endocannabinoid pathway and exerts effects including weight loss and reductions in waist circumference, together with additional improvements in some other cardiometabolic risk factors.[68–71] Rimonabant is thought to stimulate the production of adiponectin by adipocytes, which is independent of the weight loss that is also achieved. The recent Rimonabant in Obesity–Lipids (RIO–Lipids) study examined the effects of rimonabant on metabolic risk factors in obese patients.[71] Rimonabant significantly reduced body weight and waist circumference, as well as improving the profile of several cardiometabolic risk factors including atherogenic dyslipidaemia. These effects were attributed to selective CB_1-receptor blockade and appeared to be independent of weight loss alone.

From April 2006, the Quality and Outcomes Framework (QOF) of the General Medical Services (GMS) will include the development and maintenance of primary care obesity registers as a quality indicator. Unfortunately, the definition of obesity included for these purposes adopts BMI as the main measurement. As we have seen previously in this chapter, measurements of waist circumference or the waist-to-hip ratio are better indicators of abdominal obesity and thus stronger predictors of cardiometabolic risk. Moreover, BMI is only poorly correlated with the risk for CVD and diabetes. Nevertheless, the recognition of obesity in the QOF provides a welcome opportunity to encourage primary care professionals to prevent, identify and manage obesity more effectively. Hopefully, more resources will also be made available to GPs and other healthcare professionals who want to challenge the rise in obesity in the community.

References

1 Kylin E. Studien ueber das Hypertonie-Hyperglyka "mie-Hyperurika" miesyndrom. *Zentralblatt fuer Innere Medizin* 1923; **44**: 105–27.

2 Reaven GM. Banting lecture 1988. Role of insulin resistance in human disease. *Diabetes* 1988; **37**: 1595–607.

3 Alberti KG, Zimmet P, Shaw J. The metabolic syndrome – a new worldwide definition. *Lancet* 2005; **366**: 1059–62.

4 Kahn R, Buse J, Ferrannini E, Stern M. The metabolic syndrome: time for a critical appraisal: joint statement from the American Diabetes Association and the European Association for the Study of Diabetes. *Diabetes Care* 2005; **28**: 2289–304.

5 Pescatello LS, VanHeest JL. Physical activity mediates a healthier body weight in the presence of obesity. *Br J Sports Med* 2000; **34**: 86–93.

6 Sowers JR. Obesity as a cardiovascular risk factor. *Am J Med* 2003; **115(Suppl 8A)**: 37–41S.

7 Lastra-Gonzalez G, Manrique CM, Govindarajan G, Whaley-Connell A, Sowers JR. Insights into the emerging cardiometabolic prevention and management of diabetes mellitus. *Expert Opin Pharmacother* 2005; **6**: 2209–21.

8 JBS 2: Joint British Societies' guidelines on prevention of cardiovascular disease in clinical practice. *Heart* 2005; **91(Suppl 5)**: v1–52.

9 NCEP Adult Treatment Panel III. Third Report of the National Cholesterol Education Program (NCEP) Expert Panel on Detection, Evaluation, and Treatment of High Blood Cholesterol in Adults (Adult Treatment Panel III) final report. *Circulation* 2002; **106**: 3143–421.

10 World Health Organization (WHO). *Report of a WHO consultation: definition of metabolic syndrome in definition, diagnosis, and classification of diabetes mellitus and its complications. I. Diagnosis and classification of diabetes mellitus.* World Health Organization, Department of Noncommunicable Disease Surveillance: Geneva. 1999.

11 Balkau B, Charles MA. Comment on the provisional report from the WHO consultation. European Group for the Study of Insulin Resistance (EGIR). *Diabet Med* 1999; **16**: 442–3.

12 Yusuf S, Hawken S, Ounpuu S *et al*. Effect of potentially modifiable risk factors associated with myocardial infarction in 52 countries (the INTERHEART study): case-control study. *Lancet* 2004; **364**: 937–52.

13 Yusuf S, Hawken S, Ounpuu S *et al*. Obesity and the risk of myocardial infarction in 27,000 participants from 52 countries: a case-control study. *Lancet* 2005; **366**: 1640–9.

14 Ford ES, Giles WH, Dietz WH. Prevalence of the metabolic syndrome among US adults: findings from the third National Health and Nutrition Examination Survey. *JAMA* 2002; **287**: 356–9.

15 Ford ES, Giles WH, Mokdad AH. Increasing prevalence of the metabolic syndrome among US Adults. *Diabetes Care* 2004; **27**: 2444–9.

16 Lakka HM, Laaksonen DE, Lakka TA *et al*. The metabolic syndrome and total and cardiovascular disease mortality in middle-aged men. *JAMA* 2002; **288**: 2709–16.

17 Lawlor DA, Ebrahim S, Davey Smith G. The metabolic syndrome and coronary heart disease in older women: Findings from the British Women's Heart and Health Study. *Diabet Med* 2004; **21**: 906–13.

18 Ford ES, Mokdad AH, Giles WH. Trends in waist circumference among US adults. *Obes Res* 2003; **11**: 1223–31.

19 Amos AF, McCarty DJ, Zimmet P. The rising global burden of diabetes and its complications: estimates and projections to the year 2010. *Diabet Med* 1997; **14(Suppl 5)**: S1–85.

20 King H, Aubert RE, Herman WH. Global burden of diabetes, 1995–2025: prevalence, numerical estimates, and projections. *Diabetes Care* 1998; **21**: 1414–31.

21 Zimmet P, Alberti KG, Shaw J. Global and societal implications of the diabetes epidemic. *Nature* 2001; **414**: 782–7.

22 Zimmet P, Shaw J, Alberti KG. Preventing type 2 diabetes and the dysmetabolic syndrome in the real world: a realistic view. *Diabet Med* 2003; **20**: 693–702.

23 Simpson RW, Shaw JE, Zimmet PZ. The prevention of type 2 diabetes – lifestyle change or pharmacotherapy? A challenge for the 21st century. *Diabetes Res Clin Pract* 2003; **59**: 165–80.

24 Diabetes UK. *www.diabetes.org.uk*

25 National Service Framework for Diabetes: Standards (2001). *www.dh.gov.uk/PolicyAndGuidance/HealthAndSocialCareTopics/Diabetes/fs/en.*

26 World Health Organization. Factsheet – obesity and overweight, 2003. Accessed at *www.who.int/hpr/gs.fs.obesity.shtml.*

27 Harris MI. Diabetes in America: epidemiology and scope of the problem. *Diabetes Care* 1998; **21(Suppl 3)**: C11–4.

28 Mokdad AH, Bowman BA, Ford ES *et al.* The continuing epidemics of obesity and diabetes in the United States. *JAMA* 2001; **286**: 1195–200.

29 Wild S, Roglic G, Green A, Sicree R, King H. Global prevalence of diabetes: estimates for the year 2000 and projections for 2030. *Diabetes Care* 2004; **27**: 1047–53.

30 World Health Organization. *Diet, Nutrition and the Prevention of Chronic Diseases*. Geneva: World Health Organization, 2003.

31 Prentice AM, Jebb SA. Obesity in Britain: gluttony or sloth? *BMJ* 1995; **311**: 437–9.

32 Jung RT. Obesity as a disease. *Br Med Bull* 1997; **53**: 307–21.

33 The National Obesity Forum. *Healthy Weight Healthy Shape. www.nationalobesityforum.org.uk/files/content/L/6465/Booklet.pdf.*

34 National Audit Office. *Tackling Obesity in England*. London: The Stationery Office, 2001.

35 Guidelines set new definitions, update treatment for hypertension. *Bull World Health Organ* 1999; **77**: 293.

36 Burt VL, Whelton P, Roccella EJ *et al.* Prevalence of hypertension in the US adult population. Results from the Third National Health and Nutrition Examination Survey, 1988–1991. *Hypertension* 1995; **25**: 305–13.

37 Whelton PK, He J, Muntner P. Prevalence, awareness, treatment and control of hypertension in North America, North Africa and Asia. *J Hum Hypertens* 2004; **18**: 545–51.

38 Primatesta P, Brookes M, Poulter NR. Improved hypertension management and control: results from the health survey for England 1998. *Hypertension* 2001; **38**: 827–32.

39 National Quality and Outcomes Framework Statistics for England 2004/05. Bulletin: 2005/04/HSCIC. Health and Social Care Information Centre, Government Statistical Service, 2005.

40 The sixth report of the Joint National Committee on prevention, detection, evaluation, and treatment of high blood pressure. *Arch Intern Med* 1997; **157**: 2413–46.

41 Brown CD, Higgins M, Donato KA *et al.* Body mass index and the prevalence of hypertension and dyslipidemia. *Obes Res* 2000; **8**: 605–19.

42 Lawlor DA, Bedford C, Taylor M, Ebrahim S. Geographical variation in cardiovascular disease, risk factors, and their control in older women: British Women's Heart and Health Study. *J Epidemiol Community Health* 2003; **57**: 134–40.

43 Dustan HP, Roccella EJ, Garrison HH. Controlling hypertension. A research success story. *Arch Intern Med* 1996; **156**: 1926–35.

44 Klungel OH, Stricker BH, Paes AH *et al.* Excess stroke among hypertensive men and women attributable to undertreatment of hypertension. *Stroke* 1999; **30**: 1312–18.

45 Chobanian AV, Bakris GL, Black HR *et al.* The Seventh Report of the Joint National Committee on Prevention, Detection, Evaluation, and Treatment of High Blood Pressure: the JNC 7 report. *JAMA* 2003; **289**: 2560–2.

46 Waeber B. Achieving blood pressure targets in the management of hypertension. *Blood Press Suppl* 2001; **2**: 6–12.

47 Okosun IS, Prewitt TE, Cooper RS. Abdominal obesity in the United States: prevalence and attributable risk of hypertension. *J Hum Hypertens* 1999; **13**: 425–30.

48 UK Prospective Diabetes Study Group. UK Prospective Diabetes Study 27. Plasma lipids and lipoproteins at diagnosis of NIDDM by age and sex. *Diabetes Care* 1997; **20**: 1683–7.

49 Papadakis JA, Milionis HJ, Press M, Mikhailidis DP. Treating dyslipidaemia in non-insulin-dependent diabetes mellitus – a special reference to statins. *J Diabetes Complications* 2001; **15**: 211–26.

50 Austin MA, King MC, Vranizan KM, Krauss RM. Atherogenic lipoprotein phenotype. A proposed genetic marker for coronary heart disease risk. *Circulation* 1990; **82**: 495–506.

51 Steiner G. Fibrates in the metabolic syndrome and in diabetes. *Endocrinol Metab Clin North Am* 2004; **33**: 545–55.

52 Cziraky MJ. Management of dyslipidemia in patients with metabolic syndrome. *J Am Pharm Assoc (Wash DC)* 2004; **44**: 478–88.

53 Lehto S, Ronnemaa T, Haffner SM *et al.* Dyslipidemia and hyperglycemia predict coronary heart disease events in middle-aged patients with NIDDM. *Diabetes* 1997; **46**: 1354–9.

54 Turner RC, Millns H, Neil HA *et al.* Risk factors for coronary artery disease in non-insulin dependent diabetes mellitus: United Kingdom Prospective Diabetes Study (UKPDS: 23). *BMJ* 1998; **316**: 823–8.

55 Drexel H, Aczel S, Marte T *et al.* Is atherosclerosis in diabetes and impaired fasting glucose driven by elevated LDL cholesterol or by decreased HDL cholesterol? *Diabetes Care* 2005; **28**: 101–7.

56 Eckel RH, Grundy SM, Zimmet PZ. The metabolic syndrome. *Lancet* 2005; **365**: 1415–28.

57 Malik S, Wong ND, Franklin SS *et al.* Impact of the metabolic syndrome on mortality from coronary heart disease, cardiovascular disease, and all causes in United States adults. *Circulation* 2004; **110**: 1245–50.

58 Ninomiya JK, L'Italien G, Criqui MH *et al.* Association of the metabolic syndrome with history of myocardial infarction and stroke in the Third National Health and Nutrition Examination Survey. *Circulation* 2004; **109**: 42–6.

59 Doll R, Peto R. Mortality in relation to smoking: 20 years' observations on male British doctors. *BMJ* 1976; **2**: 1525–36.

60 Betteridge DJ, Morrell JM. *Clinician's Guide to Lipids and Coronary Heart Disease.* 2nd edn. London: Arnold, 2003.

61 Pouliot MC, Despres JP, Lemieux S *et al.* Waist circumference and abdominal sagittal diameter: best simple anthropometric indexes of abdominal visceral adipose tissue accumulation and related cardiovascular risk in men and women. *Am J Cardiol* 1994; **73**: 460–8.

62 Empana JP, Ducimetiere P, Charles MA, Jouven X. Sagittal abdominal diameter and risk of sudden death in asymptomatic middle-aged men: the Paris Prospective Study I. *Circulation* 2004; **110**: 2781–5.

63 Haslam D. Include measurement of waist circumference in GP contract. *BMJ* 2005; **331**: 455–6.

64 Cnop M, Havel PJ, Utzschneider KM *et al.* Relationship of adiponectin to body fat distribution, insulin sensitivity and plasma lipoproteins: evidence for independent roles of age and sex. *Diabetologia* 2003; **46**: 459–69.

65 Ross R, Janssen I. Is abdominal fat preferentially reduced in response to exercise-induced weight loss? *Med Sci Sports Exerc* 1999; **31**: S568–72.

66 Wald NJ, Law MR. A strategy to reduce cardiovascular disease by more than 80%. *BMJ* 2003; **326**: 1419.

67 Hippisley-Cox J, Coupland C. Effect of combinations of drugs on all cause mortality in patients with ischaemic heart disease: nested case-control analysis. *BMJ* 2005; **330**: 1059–63.

68 Duarte C, Alonso R, Bichet N *et al.* Blockade by the cannabinoid CB_1 receptor antagonist, rimonabant (SR141716), of the potentiation by quinelorane of food-primed reinstatement of food-seeking behavior. *Neuropsychopharmacology* 2004; **29**: 911–20.

69 Poirier B, Bidouard JP, Cadrouvele C *et al.* The anti-obesity effect of rimonabant is associated with an improved serum lipid profile. *Diabetes Obes Metab* 2005; **7**: 65–72.

70 Van Gaal LF, Rissanen AM, Scheen AJ, Ziegler O, Rossner S. Effects of the cannabinoid-1 receptor blocker rimonabant on weight reduction and cardiovascular risk factors in overweight patients: 1-year experience from the RIO-Europe study. *Lancet* 2005; **365**: 1389–97.

71 Despres JP, Golay A, Sjostrom L. Effects of rimonabant on metabolic risk factors in overweight patients with dyslipidemia. *N Engl J Med* 2005; **353**: 2121–34.

2. Improving cardiometabolic disease management

Introduction

In this chapter we offer practical advice to fellow healthcare professionals on how they can set about improving the care of patients who have various risk factors for cardiometabolic disease. This advice includes both lifestyle interventions and pharmacological or surgical interventions where appropriate. We will also consider the benefits of multiple risk factor intervention on patients' entire cardiometabolic risk profile.

The content of this section draws upon previously published articles that appeared in the publication *Improving Practice in Primary Care* (Oxford: CSF Medical Communications Ltd, 2005), written by clinicians with special interest in various elements of cardiometabolic disease management. Specifically, we consider four key clinical areas here:

- obesity
- dyslipidaemia
- hypertension
- diabetes.

As these articles represent the clinical opinions of the authors, this section remains largely unreferenced.

Obesity[b]

Summary

- Obesity is a growing clinical problem with the condition reaching epidemic proportions in the UK.
- Much of the burden of obesity management falls upon the primary care system.
- One way in which the management of obesity can be improved in practice is through the establishment of obesity clinics. However, this requires appropriate resourcing together with effective identification of relevant patients for intervention.
- Lifestyle changes, including dietary modification and introduction of regular exercise, are the starting points in weight management.
- Even modest reductions in weight can improve patients' long-term outcome.
- When lifestyle changes fail to achieve weight loss of sufficient magnitude, adjunctive drug treatment is available.

The need for obesity management

Obesity is estimated to account for a total economic burden of around £2.6 billion per annum.

Conservative estimates suggest that the direct cost to the NHS of dealing with the consequences of obesity is in the order of £0.5 billion per annum. When indirect costs are added, obesity is estimated to account for a total economic burden of around £2.6 billion per annum. Moreover, an estimated 30,000 deaths are directly attributed to obesity each year. In response to this huge (and growing) burden of obesity, the NHS has developed a number of obesity-related targets and measures. For example, obesity has been implicated in the Planning and Priorities framework for Primary Care Trusts (PCTs) 2003–2006, the National Service Frameworks (NSFs) for coronary heart disease (CHD) and diabetes, the General Medical Services (GMS) contract and the Chief Medical Officer's Report.

These developments should leave healthcare professionals in no doubt that obesity is a major health priority. Therefore, it is of considerable benefit for Primary Care Organisations (PCOs) to develop and implement

---

[b]This is an edited extract of an article written by Dr Ian Campbell, which was published in *Improving Practice in Primary Care*. Chambers, Kassianos and Morrell eds. Oxford: CSF Medical Communications Ltd, 2005.

weight management and nutrition policies as part of their overall approach to achieving these Department of Health-led goals and targets.

Overcoming practice scepticism

Many people believe that obesity does not warrant serious medical attention, maybe because of the negative way obese people are perceived. Some practice stakeholders may therefore need convincing about the merits of establishing an obesity clinic. However, the evidence of improvements in comorbid disease management and prevention is clinically and economically overwhelming, and this should help to dispel any remaining doubts about the need for prompt action. Some stakeholders may also be sceptical about the possible cost benefits of obesity management, especially for patients who require adjunctive drug treatment. However, recent guidance from the National Institute for Health and Clinical Excellence (NICE) on the use of antiobesity agents clearly outlines which patients are eligible for drug treatment, and can therefore help clinicians to achieve better weight management results with fewer comorbid complications.

Patient identification

The first step is to identify patients for whom intervention is appropriate. When identifying a patient with obesity, it is essential to consider other cardiometabolic risk factors. Many obese patients (for the purposes of this discussion defined as those patients with a body mass index [BMI] $\geq$30 kg/m^2) may also present to the surgery with other conditions such as type 2 diabetes and/or hypertension. One favoured option is to approach these patients actively during routine appointments with a view to recruiting them for weight management support and treatment. An alternative approach is to audit patients with a recorded BMI of at least 30 or those whose waist circumference exceed the ethnicity-specific cut-offs in the International Diabetes Federation (IDF) definition of the metabolic syndrome (see Chapter 1, Box 4).

> When identifying a patient with obesity, it is essential to consider other cardiometabolic risk factors.

Diagnosis

After taking an appropriate history, a number of general investigations and biochemical tests should be carried out. The results will confirm any underlying comorbidity, serve as a baseline with which to assess the patient's future progress and may serve to reassure the patient that they are theoretically able to lose weight. Such investigations should include:

- height
- weight
- BMI
- waist circumference
- blood pressure
- urinalysis
- full blood count

- thyroid function
- liver function
- lipid profile
- random blood (plasma) glucose
- fasting blood sugar.

A BMI of 25 or greater indicates that a patient is overweight whilst a BMI of 30 or more is representative of clinical obesity. Similarly, a waist circumference of 94 cm or more for men and 80 cm or higher for women (for European ethnicity), indicates a potentially serious health risk as set out in the IDF definition of the metabolic syndrome.

Patient management

Even modest weight reduction can improve a patient's quality of life and increase their life expectancy. For example, a 10% loss in weight reduces the likelihood of an obesity-related death by 20%. It can also result in a 10 mmHg fall in diastolic blood pressure, a 50% fall in fasting blood glucose, a 10% drop in total cholesterol (and a corresponding 8% increase in high density lipoprotein cholesterol [HDL-C]), and a 30% reduction in triglycerides.

Even modest weight reduction can improve a patient's quality of life and increase their life expectancy.

Lifestyle modification

The first-line intervention in obesity comprises affirmation of support, diet and lifestyle advice and behavioural therapy. A useful target for projected weight loss is 10% over a 3–6-month period, often followed by a period of weight stability, and then, if appropriate, continuation of weight loss with a further 5–10% reduction thereafter. Weekly rates of weight loss of between 0.5 and 1 kg are usually appropriate and are achievable. This will require:

- an average reduction in calorific intake of 500–600 kcal/day
- incorporation of a healthy low-fat diet
- 30 minutes of brisk exercise at least five-times weekly.

In primary care, straightforward simple advice delivered by a motivated and informed doctor or nurse is usually appropriate. If necessary, referral to a practice or community-based dietitian, where available, can also prove to be very valuable. However, if such a resource is unavailable, patients can often gain added support and advice from a reputable local weight loss group.

Patients should be encouraged to increase activity, and should aim for 30–40 minutes of additional activity on 5 days each week. Brisk walking, cycling and swimming are effective 'fat-burning' activities. Resistance exercise (e.g. free weights) increases muscle bulk and hence increases calories burnt and metabolic rate over a 24-hour period. Local exercise programmes can also be useful. In addition to its effects on promoting weight loss, regular exercise has been shown to reduce insulin resistance, lower blood pressure, reduce low density lipoprotein cholesterol (LDL-C) and triglycerides and increase HDL-C levels.

Modifying eating behaviour is an important component of weight management and altering eating habits and increasing activity levels will work in concert to provide improved prospects for long-term weight maintenance. Initial behavioural therapy should focus on giving patients sensible eating advice such as encouraging them to:

- shop for food after eating a meal
- store healthy foods where they can be seen
- use smaller plates and utensils
- eat smaller portions of food
- stop eating when full
- eat more slowly
- chew food thoroughly before swallowing.

Drug treatment

For a number of patients, diet, exercise and behavioural therapy will not be sufficient, and adjunctive therapy may be required. In these cases, two drugs are currently available – sibutramine and orlistat. Both drugs have been shown to be effective in the long-term treatment of obesity. Adjunctive drug treatment should be considered:

- after 2–6 months of compliance to dietary, behavioural and activity advice without an appropriate response
- after a failure to achieve 10% weight loss
- to achieve further reduction in symptoms
- to improve markers of comorbidity (e.g. blood glucose) and control of comorbid disease
- to improve exercise tolerance
- in cases of weight-related psychological disturbance
- to assist in weight maintenance.

Specifically, sibutramine may be best suited to a patient who has difficulty in controlling portion size, or who is unable to adapt to a low-fat diet and has been unable to demonstrate a 5% body weight loss by lifestyle change alone. Orlistat may be preferred by patients who have adopted a low-fat diet, but who need support to maintain those dietary changes and who have managed to demonstrate weight loss of at least 2.5 kg in a preceding month. With sibutramine, blood pressure and pulse need to be monitored every 2 weeks for the first 3 months, monthly for 3 months and once every 3 months thereafter. Current licensing arrangements allow for 12 months' continuous treatment with sibutramine and up to 24 months with orlistat.

Rimonabant is a recently introduced drug with a novel mode of action that directly blocks CB_1 receptor sites found in areas of the hypothalamus, liver, gastrointestinal tract, muscle and visceral fat. These receptors constitute part of a recently describe and important physiological system – the endocannabinoid system – which plays a pivotal role in the control of appetite and energy balance. Consequently, by blocking CB_1 receptors,

Regular exercise has been shown to reduce insulin resistance, lower blood pressure, reduce LDL-C and triglycerides and increase HDL-C.

For a number of patients, diet, exercise and behavioural therapy will not be sufficient, and adjunctive therapy may be required.

rimonabant helps to mediate energy balance, body weight, and lipid and glucose metabolism. A large clinical trial programme (Rimonabant in Obesity [RIO]) has investigated the effects of rimonabant compared with placebo in more than 6,600 obese and overweight patients for up to 2 years. Rimonabant-treated patients achieved significant weight loss together with a significant reduction in waist circumference. Further improvements were also reported in other cardiometabolic risk factors including HDL-C and triglyceride levels and HbA_{1C} in patients with type 2 diabetes. About half of the beneficial changes in these parameters appear to be beyond that which could be predicted from weight loss alone. Thus, the introduction of rimonabant appears to offer a useful treatment option for intervening in patients with obesity and those who are overweight with additional risk factors including type 2 diabetes and dyslipidaemia.

An example of a clinical management algorithm involving lifestyle modification and adjunctive drug treatment is shown in Figure 1.

Managing obesity in primary care – obesity clinics

It is essential that each patient participating in an obesity clinic or a surgery consultation is highly motivated (or is motivated by intervention/support) to lose weight. GPs should offer a partnership between themselves and the patients, and encourage them to attend the obesity clinic (if one is available) for at least 1 year. Realistic and achievable goals need to be established during the first appointment. Many patients have unrealistic expectations of weight loss, so it is vital to stress that even modest weight losses, followed by periods of weight maintenance, can have profound health benefits. All weight loss targets should be staggered, to help monitor gradual progress (e.g. 0.5–1 kg/week on average, with a total of 5–10% weight loss over 6 months). It is important that all members of the practice team are available for ongoing support and follow-up, as patient motivation and compliance will inevitably wane from time to time. Appointments should, at a minimum, be on a monthly basis and at each visit the patient should receive encouragement and a review of progress offered. Their new weight can be discussed and food and activity diaries reviewed, in order to encourage patients to make further changes to their diets and lifestyles where necessary. Healthy eating advice should also be provided, and the merits of regular eating patterns, low fat and smaller meal portions, and set exercise regimens should be discussed. All recommended changes must be realistic and achievable.

> It is vital to stress that even modest weight losses, followed by periods of weight maintenance, can have profound health benefits.

Throughout the course of treatment, and perhaps over a series of consultations, patients should be encouraged to:

- think about the main reasons why they have become overweight
- think about how losing weight will improve their health and quality of life
- monitor food intake by a weekly food diary (when, what and why?)

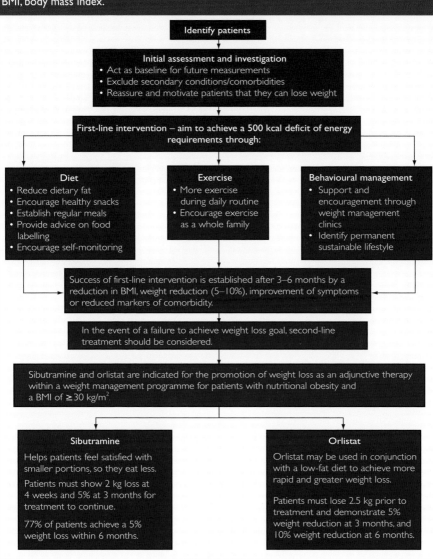

Figure 1. Clinical management of patients with obesity involving lifestyle modification and adjunctive drug treatment. Adapted from the National Obesity Forum Guidelines.[c] www.nationalobesityforum.org.uk
BMI, body mass index.

Identify patients

Initial assessment and investigation
• Act as baseline for future measurements
• Exclude secondary conditions/comorbidities
• Reassure and motivate patients that they can lose weight

First-line intervention – aim to achieve a 500 kcal deficit of energy requirements through:

Diet
• Reduce dietary fat
• Encourage healthy snacks
• Establish regular meals
• Provide advice on food labelling
• Encourage self-monitoring

Exercise
• More exercise during daily routine
• Encourage exercise as a whole family

Behavioural management
• Support and encouragement through weight management clinics
• Identify permanent sustainable lifestyle

Success of first-line intervention is established after 3–6 months by a reduction in BMI, weight reduction (5–10%), improvement of symptoms or reduced markers of comorbidity.

In the event of a failure to achieve weight loss goal, second-line treatment should be considered.

Sibutramine and orlistat are indicated for the promotion of weight loss as an adjunctive therapy within a weight management programme for patients with nutritional obesity and a BMI of ≥ 30 kg/m^2.

Sibutramine

Helps patients feel satisfied with smaller portions, so they eat less.

Patients must show 2 kg loss at 4 weeks and 5% at 3 months for treatment to continue.

77% of patients achieve a 5% weight loss within 6 months.

Orlistat

Orlistat may be used in conjunction with a low-fat diet to achieve more rapid and greater weight loss.

Patients must lose 2.5 kg prior to treatment and demonstrate 5% weight reduction at 3 months, and 10% weight reduction at 6 months.

[c]The publication of this algorithm predates the introduction of the CB$_1$ receptor antagonist, rimonabant. Consequently, this is likely to be revised in the future to include rimonabant as an additional treatment choice for the pharmacological management of obesity. Rimonabant is indicated for use as an adjunct to diet and exercise for the treatment of obese patients (body mass index [BMI] ≥30 kg/m^2) or overweight patients (BMI ≥27 kg/m^2) with associated risk factors, such as type 2 diabetes or dyslipidaemia.

It is vitally important to stress the long-term benefits of weight loss, and the need for long-term habit change throughout the programme.

- record all physical activity
- reduce fat and sugar content
- increase fruit and vegetable consumption
- reduce portion size
- develop ideas of how to increase physical activity
- reduce alcohol intake
- review their progress to date.

At each appointment the patient's weight should be checked, along with their blood pressure and waist measurement, and any pre-existing comorbid disease should also be monitored. It is vitally important to stress the long-term benefits of weight loss, and the need for long-term habit change throughout the programme.

Lipid disorders[d]

Summary

- The extent of dyslipidaemia in the UK means that the burden of lipid disorder management falls principally on primary care.
- Although new structures of care need to be developed, primary care, with its holistic and multidisciplinary approach, is well placed to meet this challenge.
- In essence, primary care needs to identify and treat populations with high global cardiovascular disease (CVD) risk in accordance with national initiatives; achieve target cholesterol and LDL-C goals; develop systems of care to ensure target delivery; foster long-term compliance; develop associated quality assurance via clinical audit.

The challenge in primary care

It is remarkable how rapidly the treatment of lipid disorders has moved from the domain of a few interested specialists to become a mainstream activity for all primary care professionals. This represents an appreciation of the burden of atherosclerotic disease in society, the realisation of the causative role of abnormal lipid levels and the emergence of incontrovertible evidence of benefit from lipid-modifying trials. The burden of CVD in the UK is large and is likely to increase as the population ages and the dual epidemics of obesity and diabetes take hold. At current rates, nearly half the population will die from a cardiovascular cause.

The treatment of lipid disorders has become a mainstream activity for all primary care professionals.

Although evidence demonstrates benefit from a level of 6% CHD risk over 10 years, current UK guidelines for primary prevention have, until recently, only endorsed intervention at the 30% 10-year level (10-year risk levels can be calculated using standard charts found at the back of the *British National Formulary* and published in other relevant management guidelines). The fiscal and workload implications for treatment to the lowest level of the evidence base are enormous and beyond the resources of most societies. Even treating to standards such as the NSF for CHD in England places a huge workload on primary care.

[d]This is an edited extract of an article written by Dr Jonathan Morrell, which was published in *Improving Practice in Primary Care*. Chambers, Kassianos and Morrell eds. Oxford: CSF Medical Communications Ltd, 2005.

In a theoretical practice of 10,000 patients, it has been estimated that 2,221 'disease control measures' will have to be performed to satisfy the requirements of the NSF for CHD in secondary prevention and in high-risk patients at the 30% 10-year risk level. When you consider that a 'disease control measure' such as achieving target blood pressure or cholesterol level might take several consultations, the workload implications for this are enormous. Despite this challenge, new recommendations identify an even lower intervention threshold at a 20% 10-year cardiovascular risk (equivalent to a 15% 10-year CHD risk) and the government is set to commit financially to the implications of full implementation.

Despite the public health importance of preventing CVD, there is evidence for an implementation gap between interventions supported by the evidence base and what happens in practice. EUROASPIRE II (European Action on Secondary and Primary Prevention by Intervention to Reduce Events) – a survey of CHD secondary prevention undertaken in 15 European countries between 1999 and 2000 – showed that 58% of patients in this high-risk group failed to reach the target for total cholesterol (<5.0 mmol/L). Many practices in the UK have subsequently worked hard at secondary prevention but considerable heterogeneity in achievement remains; it is this inequality that national initiatives are formulated to address. Therefore, the challenge for clinicians is to maximise cardiovascular prevention interventions at a level that is evidence based, pragmatic and affordable, within the direction of a national 'blueprint'.

The challenge is to maximise cardiovascular prevention interventions at a level that is evidence based, pragmatic and affordable, within the direction of a national 'blueprint'.

Lessons from the evidence base

Treating the cardiovascular risk continuum

During the last decade a series of landmark trials has established the evidence base for lipid lowering in patients across a broad spectrum of cardiovascular risk. Early clinical trials followed the clinical dichotomy of primary and secondary prevention, but gradually the concept of a global cardiovascular risk continuum began to emerge. An individual's cardiovascular risk is determined not by isolated levels of single risk factors but the composite interaction of them all. This was classically illustrated by Haffner's work in Finland, where he showed that the 7-year CHD event rate in type 2 diabetics without a prior myocardial infarction (MI) was equivalent to that in non-diabetic subjects who had already suffered an event. In other words, the risk in a primary prevention population can be as high as in patients requiring secondary prevention. It took the findings of the Heart Protection Study (HPS) to confirm that lipid-lowering therapy should be targeted to a patient's global cardiovascular risk. In this study of high-risk individuals, not only did patients with cholesterol levels below 5.0 mmol/L (or LDL-C levels below 3.0 or even 2.6 mmol/L) benefit from a statin, but they also benefited to the same degree as patients with higher entry values.

An individual's cardiovascular risk is determined not by isolated levels of single risk factors but the composite interaction of them all.

Extending intervention

In addition to the concept of targeting patients according to their level of cardiovascular risk regardless of their baseline cholesterol level, HPS also confirmed the value of lipid lowering in various patient groups not previously covered by the evidence base. Benefits were shown for women, patients over 75 years, those with atherosclerotic disease elsewhere (i.e. peripheral arterial disease and non-haemorrhagic stroke) and those with diabetes and the metabolic syndrome. The findings therefore extend the range of patients who will benefit from lipid-lowering treatment.

Lowering LDL-C

It is becoming increasingly apparent that the primary goal of lipid-lowering therapy with statins is reduction of LDL-C. Trials that demonstrate sufficient between-group LDL-C reduction show the most positive outcomes. By maintaining an average 0.96 mmol/L difference between the study groups in the HPS over 5 years, the outcomes were positive. In contrast, erosion of the LDL-C differential between groups in the lipid-lowering arm of ALLHAT (Antihypertensive and Lipid-Lowering Treatment to Prevent Heart Attack Trial) meant that it failed to achieve a positive outcome. Analysis of a Greek hospital's CHD secondary prevention activity showed that reducing LDL-C by 46% – by treating to the National Cholesterol Education Program (NCEP) LDL-C target level of less than 2.6 mmol/L – halved the subsequent cardiovascular event rate in just 3 years, compared with usual care. Aggressive LDL-C reduction observed in recent trials such as REVERSAL (Reversal of Atherosclerosis with Aggressive Lipid Lowering), PROVE-IT (Pravastatin or Atorvastatin Evaluation and Infection Therapy), ALLIANCE (Aggressive Lipid-Lowering Initiation Abates New Cardiac Events) and TNT (Treating to New Targets) confirms an enhanced clinical benefit at low target levels and underlines the decision of guideline committees to lower lipid targets to new values.

The primary goal of lipid-lowering therapy with statins is the reduction of LDL-C.

Non-HDL-C

Non-HDL-C is calculated by subtracting the concentration of HDL-C from the concentration of total cholesterol. What is left identifies not only LDL-C but also triglyceride-rich lipoproteins, which are also atherogenic (see Chapter 1). Non-HDL-C is therefore a more accurate reflection of the total atherogenic burden of the lipoprotein profile and has already been adopted by US guidelines as a secondary target of therapy in individuals with high triglycerides. It is particularly useful in patients with established vascular disease and mixed hyperlipidaemia.

Lifestyle

It must be remembered that all clinical trials using lipid-lowering drugs are performed with patients in whom lifestyle interventions have been addressed. The benefits of optimising weight, stopping smoking, increasing physical activity and eating a healthy diet are manifest. Diet alone can reduce LDL-C by more than 10% (which is in addition to the reduction achieved by drugs) and probably confers benefit through other mechanisms beyond lipid modification. Using a 'portfolio' of dietary measures (e.g. plant sterols, soya protein and viscous fibre), LDL-C has been reported to fall by 29% (Jenkins *et al. JAMA* 2003; **290**: 502–10). Unfortunately, however, lifestyle measures are poorly implemented in practice through lack of expertise, time and conviction.

The atherogenic lipoprotein profile

Many patients with CVD do not display obviously elevated LDL-C. The atherogenic lipoprotein phenotype is a term given to the dyslipidaemia characterised by low HDL-C, raised triglycerides and a shift in LDL-C structure towards a smaller, denser and a more atherogenic version of the normal particle. This change in the quality of LDL-C occurs when triglyceride levels exceed 1.5–1.7 mmol/L and is mirrored by a similar change in the quality of HDL-C, which also becomes smaller and denser and less cardioprotective.

The atherogenic lipoprotein profile is often seen in individuals with diabetes, insulin resistance or the metabolic syndrome. With the increasing prevalence of obesity and physical inactivity in our society, metabolic syndrome already has a prevalence of about 20–25%, and the future cardiovascular consequences of this are of enormous concern. Statins are not very effective in raising HDL-C levels and most statins only have relatively moderate effects on lowering triglyceride levels. As such, the 'statins for all' approach for those with this type of dyslipidaemia may not be appropriate. Most patients with the type of dyslipidaemia usually associated with type 2 diabetes or the metabolic syndrome will have normal LDL-C levels. Treatment with fibrates may be more appropriate as these are more effective in targeting the atherogenic lipid profile, but further large-scale trials are required in these patient populations. In particular, combination treatment with statins and fibrates needs to be investigated thoroughly, for safety as well as for efficacy outcomes.

Drug treatment

Treating to global cardiovascular risk means applying the range of cardiovascular prevention interventions appropriate for each individual. Clearly, this means optimising blood pressure and glycaemic control, as well as the lipid profile, and using antiplatelet drugs where appropriate. Prescribing analyses show that most practitioners will use statins.

Table 1. Implications of targeting statin treatment at four coronary heart disease (CHD) risk levels, showing the number needed to treat (NNT), cost-effectiveness and implications for the UK population. (From Pickin *et al.* Heart 1999; **82**: 325–32.)

| | 10-year CHD risk level | | | |
	45%	30%	20%	5%
NNT (over 5 years)[a]	13	20	30	40
Cost per life-year gained (£)	5,100	8,200	10,700	12,500
UK adults above threshold (%)	5.1	8.2	15.8	24.7
Annual cost (£ million)	549	885	1712	2673

[a]NNT for 5 years to prevent one major coronary event.

The growing evidence base for the statins has allowed a more rigorous assessment of their cost-effectiveness; data looking at different CHD risk thresholds are shown in Table 1. In comparison with many other valued healthcare interventions, the cost-effectiveness of statins is within the NICE 'benchmark' for cost per life-years gained and this explains the commitment of central government to fund their use. The trials show that, to be effective, statins need to be continued for several years before affecting outcomes; the challenge of ensuring appropriate follow-up and compliance is another task for primary care.

> The challenge of ensuring appropriate follow-up and compliance is another task for primary care.

Meeting the challenges in practice

Patient identification

Reacting to both best practice and national initiatives, primary care teams have already begun to identify patients with established CVD for intervention. Most GPs have concentrated on patients with established CHD but this strategy could easily be extended to include patients with peripheral arterial disease, ischaemic stroke and diabetes, whose absolute risk of a further cardiovascular event is also high. The huge numbers of people requiring primary prevention assessment poses a major challenge to the primary care workload but a pragmatic start would be to offer risk assessment to those patients with metabolic syndrome, hypertension or a family history of premature vascular disease.

> A pragmatic start would be to offer risk assessment to those patients with metabolic syndrome, hypertension or a family history of premature vascular disease.

Patient assessment

In secondary prevention, the decision to treat is straightforward. Diabetes should be treated as a CHD risk-equivalent. In some cases, life expectancy and comorbidity enter the equation, and this is particularly relevant when assessing the elderly. In primary prevention, the 10-year cardiovascular event risk can be calculated using Framingham-based risk function charts, such as those produced by the Joint British Societies (JBS) and the British Hypertension Society (BHS). A computerised version of the mathematical function allows a more precise calculation. Intervention is currently recommended at the 20% 10-year CVD threshold (equivalent to 15% 10-year CHD risk). Patients whose 10-year CVD risk is 10–20% remain at increased risk, and because the evidence base suggests treatment benefit, the UK government has sanctioned the sale of simvastatin direct to consumers under pharmacist control.

An important feature of the assessment of abnormal lipid levels is to exclude causes of secondary hyperlipidaemia. Commonly these include obesity, diabetes and excessive alcohol intake. Fasting blood glucose, liver function tests and measurement of thyroid stimulating hormone are useful investigations before initiating treatment.

Developing structured care

The existence of the implementation gap between expectation and reality underlines the failure, in many practices, to develop systematic pathways of care for patients needing CVD prevention interventions. The computer is central to the efforts of most successful practices, and appropriate coding, database construction, and the use of templates and call and recall systems all enhance the delivery of care. Much research has focused on the role of the primary care nurse, and data from the Grampian region in Scotland show significant improvements in the level of interventions and even the death rate at 4.7 years in CHD patients attending nurse-led clinics.

Nurses already have established roles in chronic disease management in asthma and diabetes in primary care. As the aims are so similar, a logical step would be to expand diabetes clinics into CVD prevention clinics. Clearly, extra resources will be needed, but revenue from new contractual arrangements for GPs might facilitate this. PCOs will co-ordinate local activities and facilitate integration with secondary care services. The role of intermediate-care GP 'specialists' is also likely to expand.

Lipid targets

The NSF CHD targets suggest that total cholesterol should be reduced to less than 5.0 mmol/L (or by 25%, whichever is greater) and LDL-C to less than 3.0 mmol/L (or by 30%, whichever is greater). Despite their relative simplicity, these targets are still poorly interpreted, to the disadvantage of some patients.

The majority of clinicians aim to achieve the headline total cholesterol target and pay little attention to LDL-C, the concept of percentage reduction or the subtleties of the lipoprotein profile. This approach is further perpetuated by the GMS contract which currently only rewards total cholesterol achievements.

Until direct LDL-C measurement becomes widely available, LDL-C

The majority of clinicians aim to achieve the headline total cholesterol target and pay little attention to LDL-C, the concept of percentage reduction or the subtleties of the lipoprotein profile.

must be calculated mathematically using the Friedewald equation. As this requires the additional measurement of both HDL-C and triglycerides, the fasting profile is required, with attendant inconvenience to both patient and practice. In addition, some GPs are denied access to full fasting lipid profiles by their laboratories. Nevertheless, as LDL-C is the major lipoprotein involved in atherosclerotic plaque formation, a better predictor of CHD and the major target of statins, it is logical to have this as the major target. Situations exist, particularly in patients with low HDL-C, where target cholesterol may be reached but not target LDL-C. In the USA, NCEP guidelines are couched in terms of LDL-C and do not refer to total cholesterol levels.

Percentage reduction was introduced as a concept to ensure satisfactory reductions of total cholesterol and LDL-C in treated patients. The lessons from trials show us, for example, that treating a patient with an initial cholesterol level of 5.1 mmol/L and achieving a result of 4.9 mmol/L is unlikely to produce much benefit. For such a patient, the percentage-reduction strategy would be more beneficial and more in keeping with the evidence base. Using percentage reduction in target setting is difficult to audit, however, and is rarely undertaken in primary care.

New recommendations from the JBS (JBS 2) identify lower targets for total cholesterol (<4.0 mmol/L or a 25% reduction) and LDL-C (<2.0 mmol/L or a 30% reduction). The JBS guidelines have also lowered the audit standards (total cholesterol <5 mmol/L or a 25% reduction; LDL-C <3.0 mmol/L or a 30% reduction). The JBS guidelines state that HDL-C and triglyceride values should be considered in overall lipid management. Targets have not been set for these lipid fractions but the JBS provides 'desirable values' for non-HDL-C (<3.0 mmol/L), triglycerides (<1.7 mmol/L) and HDL-C (>1.0 mmol/L for men and >1.2 mmol/L for women).

With the current fixation on achieving lipid targets, it should be borne in mind that the targets are derived by consensus panels and have little evidence from clinical outcome trials *per se*. Many patients in clinical trials failed to achieve target levels, yet, presumably, derived benefit from treatment. Prescribers must therefore weigh up the benefit from the specific settings of randomised trials with the extrapolated benefit derived from the relative surrogate of achieving target lipid values.

Strategies to achieve target lipid levels

Most commonly, GPs are choosing a target-based strategy. Although their efficacy varies, statins are all highly effective in reducing total cholesterol and LDL-C. The more potent statins and new combination drugs reduce cholesterol more and therefore more patients reach target concentrations at starter doses. Many GPs prefer the ease of this approach to dose-titration, which may involve more patient visits.

Whatever strategy is chosen, all practitioners will encounter patients in whom target lipid levels are not being achieved and as guideline targets are reduced further, this will become increasingly commonplace. Possible solutions include:

- checking compliance
- checking dietary adherence
- titrating statin (each dose-doubling reduces LDL-C by 6%)
- switching statin
- adding a plant sterol or stanol to the diet
- combination therapy (usually ezetimibe, sometimes a fibrate or nicotinic acid)
- referral to a lipid specialist.

Quality assurance

The importance and ease of clinical audit of cholesterol measurements has made them ideal quality indicators within the new contractual frameworks for primary care.

The importance and ease of clinical audit of cholesterol measurements has made them ideal quality indicators within the new contractual frameworks for primary care. In the secondary prevention of CHD, seven quality points are available for ensuring that 90% of CHD patients have a cholesterol recording over the preceding 15 months, and 17 quality points are available if 70% achieve the total cholesterol target of 5.0 mmol/L or below over the same time period. The same standards and time frames apply for cerebrovascular disease and diabetes, with two and three points available, respectively, for measurement, and five and six points, respectively, for target achievement (upper threshold of 60% for cerebrovascular disease).

Primary healthcare professionals need to develop appropriately structured care to facilitate easy recording of data, and built-in audits can update automatically when chronologically programmed to ensure that the quality standards are met.

Hypertension[e]

Summary

- Hypertension is a significant problem both in the UK and globally, and its management is a major part of GPs' daily workload.
- Despite the fact that uncontrolled hypertension places patients at a greater risk of CVD and death, its management in primary care remains suboptimal.
- Initiatives aiming to improve the management of hypertension in the UK include the GMS contract. A significant proportion of clinical points in the GMS contract are related directly to the management of hypertension.
- The BHS guidelines call for treatment initiation at certain thresholds determined by the magnitude of blood pressure elevation, the level of cardiovascular risk and the presence or absence of other comorbid conditions such as diabetes.
- In order for patients to achieve new and more stringent blood pressure targets, multiple drug treatment is likely to be needed.
- The GMS contract has driven the need for effective clinical audit, particularly with regard to performance in the control of hypertension.
- Given conflicts in the BHS and NICE guideline recommendations, and emerging clinical data, a joint committee (with representatives from NICE and the BHS) has undertaken to review the recent guidelines on hypertension.

Disease burden

The World Health Organization (WHO) has identified hypertension as one of the most important preventable causes of premature morbidity and mortality in developed and developing countries. It affects about 1 billion people worldwide and is the most common treatable risk factor for CVD in patients over 50 years of age. If we accept that a blood

[e]This is an edited extract of an article written by Dr Mark Davis, which was published in *Improving Practice in Primary Care*. Chambers, Kassianos and Morrell eds. Oxford: CSF Medical Communications Ltd, 2005.

pressure above 140/90 mmHg requires cardiovascular risk calculation as a minimum requirement, which may necessitate the initiation of treatment, there are an estimated 42% of people aged 35–64 years with a blood pressure above this level. When we consider patients over 60 years then 70% will have hypertension. The majority of this latter group of patients will have isolated systolic hypertension.

Hypertension clusters with other risk factors

We are now encouraged to calculate overall cardiovascular risk in patients with hypertension by identifying multiple risk factors and then intervening appropriately.

People with hypertension often have a clustering of additional risk factors for CVD. These include dyslipidaemia, impaired glucose tolerance (IGT) and central obesity, which, together with hypertension, are hallmarks of the metabolic syndrome. As a result of this clustering of risk factors, the treatment of blood pressure in isolation will leave patients at an unacceptably high risk of cardiovascular complications and death. Consequently, we are now encouraged to calculate overall cardiovascular risk in patients with hypertension by identifying multiple risk factors and then intervening appropriately.

Meta-analyses of large-scale randomised controlled trials have demonstrated that reductions in systolic blood pressure (SBP) of 10–14 mmHg and in diastolic blood pressure (DBP) of 5–6 mmHg lower the incidence of stroke by two-fifths and CHD by one-fifth. The evidence base for the benefits of intervention in patients with high blood pressure gives us an obligation to improve our management of hypertension, though the number of patients involved represents a continuing and significant challenge for professionals working in primary care. National surveys continue to highlight the fact that there is still substantial underdiagnosis, undertreatment and poor rates of blood pressure control within the UK, though recent performance data from the quality and outcomes framework (QOF) of the GMS contract show signs that situation is slowly improving.

The challenges facing primary care

We are in the fortunate position of having access to a number of clear and practical guidelines for the management of hypertension. In 2004, the BHS published its fourth set of guidelines (Guidelines for Management of Hypertension: The Report of the Fourth Working Party of the British Hypertension Society 2004 [BHS IV]. *J Hum Hypertens* 2004; **18**: 139–85). A user-friendly version of these guidelines was also published in the *British Medical Journal* (*BMJ* 2004; **328**: 634–40). These guidelines are intended for GPs, practice nurses and generalists in hospital.

New systems of healthcare delivery will be needed to ensure that these guidelines are implemented in primary care. We will not be successful unless multidisciplinary teams work in a systematic and structured way to advise, educate and support our patients. There will also need to be a move away from rigid clinic-based care towards greater use of remote centres such as pharmacies. There is clearly also a need for the extended role provided by nurse practitioners, pharmacists and other healthcare professionals if we are to build the foundations for a service that enables widespread and effective detection, monitoring and treatment of high blood pressure and its associated increased risk of CVD.

New systems of healthcare delivery will be needed to ensure that these guidelines are implemented in primary care.

Initiatives to improve hypertension management – BHS *vs* NICE?

PCTs have an important role in supporting and enhancing primary care. They will also take the lead in the development of new types of service delivery. The Department of Health has provided the lead in the prevention of CVD through its NSFs in England (in particular the NSFs for CHD, diabetes and older people). There are also similar initiatives in Scotland and Wales. The NSFs suggest that we prioritise our efforts by optimally treating hypertension in those at greatest risk of CVD. This includes those people with existing occlusive vascular disease and diabetes. They also support our efforts to identify those who have yet to exhibit manifest occlusive vascular disease but who, because of multiple risk factors, are at high risk of CVD.

The GMS contract, first introduced in 2003, is an important step towards the development of primary care in the UK. The quality framework has a significant leaning towards CVD prevention and management and, as such, the detection and management of hypertension features strongly. The payment consequent upon achieving the quality indicators should encourage practices to improve hypertension management and will reward them for delivering quality care. Of the 655 clinical points available in the GMS contract (from April 2006), 148 relate directly to hypertension. A further 15 points out of the 181 organisational points available also relate to hypertension.

NICE has also prepared guidance for the management of hypertension, which was published in August 2004, several months after publication of the revised BHS guidelines. For many years recommendations from the BHS have been accepted as best practice throughout the UK. What, then, does the NICE guideline add to the latest BHS guidelines, and how important are the differences in interpretation? In many respects the advice is similar and differences are only minor. However, this begs the question, why publish NICE guidelines so soon after the BHS guidelines? Was it essential that NICE set slightly less stringent targets for most patients' treatment (BHS ≤140/85 mmHg; NICE ≤140/90 mmHg)? The most alarming difference is in the management of patients, with both organisations agreeing that lifestyle modifications should be the first step, but NICE giving undue prominence to procedures of little utility such as relaxation therapy. Moreover, when it comes to drug therapy, NICE reverts to diuretic-based stepped-care therapy for all regardless of age and ethnicity.

recommended the ABCD algorithm for drug treatment (see later in this section), and clinicians were just getting used to this approach when NICE suggested an alternative. Perhaps it is just coincidence that NICE currently recommends treatment with drugs that are the least expensive and that are available in non-proprietary formulations?

NICE have recently agreed to revise their guidelines – several years earlier than was planned – in conjunction with the BHS. This is in the light of results of the Anglo–Scandinavian Cardiac Outcome Trial (ASCOT) which evaluated combinations of modern antihypertensive drugs compared with older regimens. Hopefully, this will produce a more clinically driven set of guidelines, less emphasis on short-term drug acquisition costs and also help to avoid the confusing duplication of activities and conflicting recommendations. In the meantime the substantive recommendations in this section are based on the most recent published BHS guidelines.

Practical advice to meet these challenges

Nobody working in primary care will underestimate the size of the challenge that we have been set. Practices will be able to identify those patients in whom blood pressure control is desirable by using existing disease registers. Patients with existing CVD should be identifiable from our CHD and stroke registers. They should then be subject to regular review, and by using practice protocols and templates that are readily available on our IT systems, it should be possible to Read code all the actions that we take.

Once our actions are Read coded it should be relatively straightforward to undertake a search and identify those whose blood pressure is not to target. Patients with diabetes should also be added to our 'secondary prevention' remit. Diabetics are also likely to be hypertensive and as such, the targets that are set for diabetics are particularly challenging. The thresholds and targets for intervention in hypertension taken from the BHS guidelines are set out in Box 1.

Many of our patients with hypertension will not yet be known to us. The GMS contract encourages us to record blood pressure in patients aged over 45 years at a minimum of 5-year intervals. This is good practice and can be done opportunistically either by GPs or by nursing staff. It is also likely that an increasing number of pharmacists will offer blood pressure screening as part of their service, and if this information is transmitted to the practices, this will help us enormously in our task.

A management algorithm supported by the new BHS guidelines for patients with different levels of blood pressure is presented in Figure 2. This algorithm indicates that patients with a sustained blood pressure above 160/100 mmHg should receive treatment no matter what other risk factors are present. An SBP of 140–160 mmHg and a DBP of 90–100 mmHg warrant further risk assessment. A sustained blood pressure within these parameters would necessitate treatment if there is target organ damage or CVD complications, or if the patient has diabetes or a

Practices will be able to identify those patients in whom blood pressure control is desirable by using existing disease registers.

> **Box 1.** Thresholds and treatment targets for antihypertensive drug treatment. Adapted from Williams *et al. BMJ* 2004; **328**: 634–40. CVD, cardiovascular disease; DBP, diastolic blood pressure; SBP, systolic blood pressure.
>
> - Antihypertensive treatment should be initiated in patients with sustained SBP ≥160 mmHg or sustained DBP ≥100 mmHg despite non-pharmacological measures.
>
> - Antihypertensive treatment should be initiated in patients with SBP 140–159 mmHg or sustained DBP 90–99 mmHg if target organ damage is present, or there is evidence of CVD or diabetes, or where the 10-year CVD risk is ≥20%.
>
> - For most patients, the recommended blood pressure target is ≤140/85 mmHg. In those with diabetes, renal impairment or established CVD, a lower target of ≤130/80 mmHg is recommended.
>
> - When using ambulatory blood pressure readings, mean daytime pressures are preferable (this value should be approximately 10/5 mmHg lower than office blood pressure equivalent for thresholds and targets). Similar adjustments are required for averages of home blood pressure readings.

10-year risk of CVD of 20% or above. CVD complications or target organ damage include:
- stroke, transient ischaemic attack, dementia, carotid bruits
- left ventricular hypertrophy or left ventricular strain on ECG
- heart failure
- myocardial infarction, angina, coronary artery bypass graft or angioplasty
- fundal haemorrhages or exudates, papilloedema
- proteinuria
- renal impairment (raised creatinine).

There are various validated ways of calculating cardiovascular risk but the most commonly used are those recommended in the JBS guidelines. These have recently been updated and simplified and allow for calculation of CVD, rather than CHD risk, to reflect the importance of stroke prevention as well as CHD prevention. The BHS has also published these tables in its guidelines. If patients with mild-to-moderate hypertension do not fulfil the above criteria then it is adequate to reassess their blood pressure and CVD risk annually. Blood pressures below 140/90 mmHg do not require intervention.

In our hypertensive patients we should also undertake the following routine investigations:
- urine strip tests for protein and blood
- serum creatinine and electrolytes
- blood glucose levels (ideally fasting blood glucose)
- serum lipid profile (HDL-C and total cholesterol at the very least; fasted profile required for triglycerides)
- ECG.

Figure 2. British Hypertension Society guidelines for the management of hypertension. Adapted from Williams *et al. BMJ* 2004; **328**: 634–40.
[a]Unless malignant phase of hypertensive emergency, confirm over 1–2 weeks then treat.
[b]If CV complications, target organ damage, or diabetes are present, confirm over 3–4 weeks then treat; if absent remeasure weekly and treat if blood pressure persists at this level over 4–12 weeks.
[c]If CV complications, target organ damage, or diabetes are present, confirm over 3–4 weeks then treat; if absent remeasure monthly and treat if this level is maintained and if estimated 10-year CVD risk is ≥20%.
[d]Assessed with risk chart for CVD.
CV, cardiovascular, CVD cardiovascular disease.

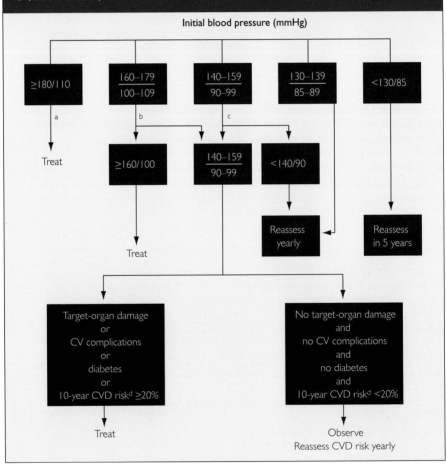

The target blood pressure for most patients is 140/85 mmHg or lower (Box 1). For patients with diabetes, renal impairment or established CVD, a lower target of below 130/80 mmHg is recommended. It is accepted that even with optimal treatment, some patients will not be able to achieve these targets. Because of this, a minimum audit standard has been set which is under 150/90 mmHg in most patients and below 140/80 mmHg in those at the highest risk.

Disease management

Lifestyle changes

Advice on lifestyle changes should be provided to all patients who are being considered for pharmacological interventions. There is some evidence that lifestyle modification can prevent those with borderline or high–normal blood pressures becoming hypertensive and thus requiring treatment. The lifestyle measures that have been shown to lower blood pressure and reduce the rise of blood pressure with age are shown in Box 2.

We know that certain lifestyle measures reduce the risk of CVD, and these include smoking cessation and reducing the intake of total and saturated fats and their replacement with monounsaturated fats such as olive oil. To succeed with lifestyle change members of the practice team need to acquire the skills and enthusiasm that are required to achieve behaviour modification. Considerable time will need to be spent with patients and other family members in order to give them the best advice as to how lifestyle change can be achieved.

> To succeed with lifestyle change members of the practice team need to acquire the skills and enthusiasm that are required to achieve behaviour modification.

Drug treatment

In general, the main determinant of benefit from antihypertensive drugs is the magnitude of the blood pressure reduction that is achieved rather than the choice of therapy. Although there is only minimal evidence for

---

Box 2. Lifestyle measures to lower blood pressure. Adapted from Williams et al. BMJ 2004; **328**: 634–40. BMI, body mass index.

- Maintenance of normal body weight (BMI 20–25 kg/m^2).
- Reduce salt intake to below 100 mmol/day (equivalent to less than 6 g of NaCl or less than 2.4 g of Na+ per day).
- Limit alcohol consumption (males: ≤3 units/day; females: ≤2 units/day).[a]
- Engage in regular aerobic physical exercise (e.g. brisk walking) for at least 30 minutes each day on most days of the week, and at least 3 days of the week.
- Consume at least five portions of fresh fruit and vegetables daily.
- Reduce the intake of total and saturated fat.

[a]A unit is equivalent to 10 mL of pure alcohol.

differences between classes of drugs with regard to cardiovascular outcomes, there are a number of important caveats to this. For example, calcium-channel blocker based therapy may be less protective than other agents with regard to the development of heart failure, though some small benefits have been reported with regard to stroke prevention. The Losartan Intervention For Endpoint Reduction in Hypertension (LIFE) study has demonstrated even larger benefits for angiotensin II receptor antagonist therapy over β-blocker therapy with regard to stroke prevention, despite broadly similar blood pressure reductions being achieved with both agents. Data from ASCOT recently showed that contemporary agents offer greater benefits in terms of cardiovascular outcomes compared with first-generation drugs. Finally, there can be compelling indications and compelling contraindications to different drugs in very specific groups of patients (for specific detailed recommendations see the BHS guidelines).

Should none of these special considerations apply, the choice of drug therapy should follow the ABCD algorithm as suggested by the BHS. The theory underpinning this algorithm is that hypertension can be broadly classified as high renin or low renin, and is therefore best treated initially with one of the two categories of hypertensive drugs. This tends to be age and race dependent.

The classes of drugs within the ABCD algorithm are:

- angiotensin-converting enzyme (ACE) inhibitors or angiotensin II receptor antagonists
- β-blockers
- calcium-channel blockers
- diuretics.

Drugs in the A and B classes inhibit the renin–angiotensin system, whilst those in the C and D classes do not. Patients who are younger than 55 years and Caucasian should be started on A or B drugs whilst patients over 55 years or of Afro-Caribbean origin should start on C or D drugs (Figure 3). As most people require more than one drug to control blood pressure it is usual that step 2 will be reached and this will involve the combination of an A or B drug with a C or D drug. The BHS recommends caution when using a B and D combination in patients at especially high risk of developing diabetes. This caution is justified given the availability of trial evidence, which indicates that this combination results in an increased incidence of new onset diabetes.

There is general agreement that the agent used should ideally be effective for 24 hours when taken as a once-daily dose. Unless it is necessary to lower blood pressure urgently, an interval of at least 4 weeks should be allowed to observe a full response before altering the treatment regimen.

To reach the revised targets, the majority of patients will require combination therapy.

Most drugs provide similar blood pressure reductions. The placebo-adjusted reductions for patients with baseline blood pressures of about 160/95 mmHg are approximately 10/5 mmHg. Thus, to reach the revised targets, the majority of patients will require combination therapy.

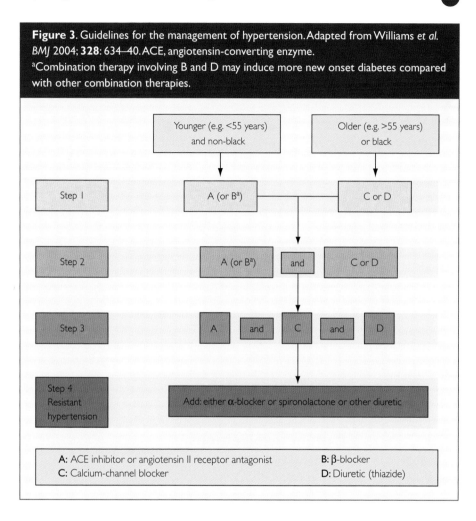

Figure 3. Guidelines for the management of hypertension. Adapted from Williams *et al.* *BMJ* 2004; **328**: 634–40. ACE, angiotensin-converting enzyme.
[a]Combination therapy involving B and D may induce more new onset diabetes compared with other combination therapies.

It is likely that most of the management of hypertension within a practice setting will be carried out by nurses working to a practice protocol which should make it clear when patients need to be referred to a GP. Similarly GPs should be clear as to when they should consider referral for a specialist opinion. The BHS indications for specialist referral are summarised in Box 3.

As hypertension is only one of a number of cardiovascular risk factors that can coexist in this patient population, the BHS also provides guidance on the use of statins and aspirin in both primary and secondary prevention patient populations.

Box 3. Indications for specialist referral. Adapted from Williams *et al. BMJ* 2004; **328**: 634–40.

Urgent treatment required
- Accelerated hypertension (severe hypertension and retinopathy [grade III–IV])
- Severe hypertension (>220/120 mmHg)
- Impending complications (e.g. transient ischaemic attack, left ventricular failure)

Possible underlying cause
- Any clue in history or examination of a secondary cause (e.g. hypokalaemia with increased or high–normal plasma sodium [Conn's syndrome])
- Elevated creatinine
- Proteinuria or haematuria
- Sudden onset or worsening of hypertension
- Resistance to multidrug regimen (at least three drugs)
- Young age (<20 years: any hypertension; <30 years: needing treatment)

Therapeutic problems
- Multiple drug intolerance
- Multiple drug contraindications
- Persistent non-adherence or non-compliance

Special situations
- Unusual blood pressure variability
- White coat hypertension
- Hypertension in pregnancy

Patient involvement

An essential component of successful blood pressure management is to obtain the active participation of each individual. This can be achieved in a number of ways.

- Patients with high blood pressure should be involved in the decision as to what lifestyle changes they need to take, and whether drug therapy is appropriate.
- The likely risk reduction obtained as a consequence of antihypertensive treatment should be understood.
- Patients should be aware of the likelihood that they will need to take two or three drugs to achieve sufficient reductions in blood pressure, and be conscious of the possible side-effects that they may encounter.
- Wherever possible a written treatment plan should be drawn up and agreed with the patient.
- With modern semi-automated blood pressure machines it is possible to involve more patients in the measurement of their own blood pressure, which can save visits to a primary healthcare team. However, it is important to remember that the targets are based on

'clinic' blood pressures and home measurements will usually be lower. A correction factor of 10/5 mmHg should be applied when considering home results.

- Individual patients can obtain information directly from the Blood Pressure Association (*www.bpassoc.org.uk*).

Clinical audit

It is now essential that interventions relating to blood pressure control are recorded electronically. The survival of practices in the age of performance management means that electronic audit is no longer optional. We need to ensure that the templates that we use are correctly Read coded, thereby enabling the information to be retrieved easily from our systems. It seems likely that many practices will use the quality indicators in the GMS contract as a basis for their audit. Programmes which interrogate our databases, such as the Population Manager in the EMIS system, will enable the monitoring of our progress towards quality points. Correct Read coding will also enable individual practices to undertake more sophisticated searches should they so wish.

Conclusions

It is in the interests of each practice, as well as in the interest of the population that it serves, that we make real progress in reducing blood pressure in our patient population and thereby reduce their cardiovascular risk. As more trial evidence emerges, current guidance will be modified further.

The detection and treatment of high blood pressure and its associated CVD risk will continue to be a key focus of healthcare policy in the UK. We should continue to assess the need for treatment on the basis of absolute risk. The ongoing reorganisation of healthcare within the UK and the emphasis on clinical audit, quality of care and improvements in the systems of care provides us with an excellent opportunity to deliver improved hypertension management and thereby reduce the burden of CVD.

The detection and treatment of high blood pressure and its associated CVD risk will continue to be a key focus of healthcare policy in the UK.

Diabetes, glycaemic control and comorbid disorders[f]

Summary

- The increasing prevalence of type 2 diabetes has resulted in a greater workload in primary care.
- GPs are bombarded with guidelines and targets for the treatment of patients with diabetes, particularly arising from the GMS contract and the NSF.
- The GMS contract awards up to 93 points for the management of diabetes, reflecting the seriousness with which diabetes and its comorbid conditions are regarded.
- Ten practical strategies, outlined in this section, can be used to meet these targets.
- A holistic approach is recommended, including measurement of glycaemic control, BMI, hypertension, dyslipidaemia and other factors.
- The identification of patients with impaired states of glucose metabolism and advocating diet and exercise in these cases may help prevent the progression to diabetes.

Signposts to optimal care

The WHO predicts that by 2010 there will be 3 million sufferers of diabetes in the UK.

The world is faced with an epidemic of diabetes. The WHO predicts that by 2010 there will be 3 million sufferers of diabetes in the UK. The increasing prevalence of the condition, particularly of type 2 diabetes, is reflected in a greater primary care workload. For practitioners seeking to provide optimal care, there are a number of influences which have made themselves apparent over the past few years:

- evidence-based medicine
- therapeutic targets
- the NSF for diabetes
- the GMS contract.

---

[f]This is an edited extract of an article written by Dr Eugene Hughes, which was published in *Improving Practice in Primary Care*. Chambers, Kassianos and Morrell eds. Oxford: CSF Medical Communications Ltd, 2005.

Evidence-based medicine

We are awash with evidence to support our management of diabetes. The Diabetes Control and Complications Trial (DCCT) and UKPDS studies clarified our understanding of the progress of type 1 diabetes and type 2 diabetes respectively. The Scandinavian Simvastatin Survival Study (4S), West of Scotland Coronary Prevention Study (WOSCOPS) and HPS pointed the way in lipid management, and the Hypertension Optimal Treatment (HOT) study, Heart Outcomes Prevention (HOPE) trial and ALLHAT have enabled
us to logically assess antihypertensive therapy. More recently, the Collaborative Atorvastatin Diabetes Study (CARDS) has strengthened the case for the use of statins as primary prevention in type 2 diabetes. ASCOT has raised important questions about the choice of therapeutic agents in hypertension. The long-awaited PROACTVE study (Prospective Pioglitazone Clinical Trial in Macrovascular Events) suggests that oral antidiabetic therapy may have beneficial effects on some cardiovascular outcomes.

Therapeutic targets

As a result of the previously mentioned studies, the 2005 guidelines of the JBS have established some treatment targets for diabetes (Box 4).

The NSF for diabetes

2001 saw the publication of the *National Service Framework for Diabetes: Standards* document. It was followed a year later by *National Service Framework for Diabetes: Delivery Strategy*. Together, these documents set out a 10-year strategy for PCTs with some important milestones, setting out 12 standards to be reached by 2013.

Box 4. The Joint British Societies (JBS 2) recommended treatment targets for type 2 diabetes.

Parameter	Target
Fasting plasma glucose	<6.0 mmol/L
HbA_{1C}	≤6.5%
Blood pressure	130/80 mmHg
Total cholesterol	<4.0 mmol/L (or 25% reduction)
LDL-C	<2.0 mmol/L (or 25% reduction)
HDL-C	>1.2 mmol/L (women) and >1.0 mmol/L (men)
Triglycerides	<1.7 mmol/L

HbA_{1C}, glycated haemoglobin; HDL-C, high density lipoprotein cholesterol; LDL-C, low density lipoprotein cholesterol.

The GMS contract

Targets have now become a way of life for GPs. We have become accustomed to the money-for-points concept of the GMS contract. From April 2006, new points are being introduced for obesity and extra points for diabetes in recognition of the workload involved. In addition, lower thresholds of the payment stages will change. This will effectively mean more work for the same money, as there will be less room for manoeuvre. On a positive note, there are also extra points for assessing depression in people with diabetes.

Practical strategies to improve practice

Faced with all these possible directions, how should we proceed? Is it possible to adopt a practice strategy that can unify all the above components? By focusing on the quality indicators in the GMS contract we can:

● make best use of the available evidence
● allow us to strive to achieve therapeutic targets
● adhere to the principles of the NSF
● earn maximum points under the new contract.

Practice register

This is currently worth six points. You are required to set up a register of all patients (type 1 and type 2 diabetes) for systematic care, recall and audit purposes. The rules do not specify how the diagnosis should be made, but it would seem sensible to follow the WHO criteria (Table 3). Most practices will have already created a register of all patients with diabetes. The register is going to be the focus for obtaining all the other points, so it is important to get it right. All patients with diabetes should be on the register, and all people on the register should have diabetes. This may sound self-evident, but I found several people with a computer diagnosis of diabetes where assumptions had been made, and even one where the diagnosis related to another family member as in 'diagnosis DIABETES' – then in free text –'mother has it!'

BMI

Three points for a record of BMI in the preceding 15 months. Remember that patients frequently get weighed at hospital appointments – it is important to be able to utilise data from various sources. A trained clerk can process all communications from clinics and extract the necessary data. Weight control in overweight patients with diabetes is associated with improved glycaemic control. With eight points now being awarded for an obesity register, this assumes even greater importance.

Table 2. Indicators for patients with either type 1 or type 2 diabetes.

Diabetes mellitus (diabetes)

This set of indicators refers to patients with both type 1 and type 2 diabetes

Indicator	Points	Payment stages
Records		
DM 19. The practice can produce a register of all patients aged 17 years and older with diabetes mellitus, which specifies whether the patient has type 1 or type 2 diabetes.	6	
Outgoing Management		
DM 2. The percentage of patients with diabetes whose notes record BMI in the previous 15 months.	3	40–90%
DM 5. The percentage of patients with diabetes who have a record of HbA_{1C} or equivalent in the previous 15 months.	3	40–90%
DM 20. The percentage of patients with diabetes in whom the last HbA_{1C} is 7.5 or less (or equivalent test/reference range depending on local laboratory) in last 15 months.	17	40–50%
DM 7. The percentage of patients with diabetes in whom the last HbA_{1C} is 10 or less (or equivalent test/reference range depending on local laboratory) in last 15 months.	11	40–90%
DM 21. The percentage of patients with diabetes who have a record of retinal screening in the previous 15 months.	5	40–90%
DM 9. The percentage of patients with diabetes with a record of the presence or absence of peripheral pulses in the previous 15 months.	3	40–90%
DM 10. The percentage of patients with diabetes with a record of neuropathy testing in the previous 15 months.	3	40–90%
DM 11. The percentage of patients with diabetes who have a record of their blood pressure in the previous 15 months.	3	40–90%
DM 12. The percentage of patients with diabetes in whom the last blood pressure is 145/85 or less.	18	40–60%
DM 13. The percentage of patients with diabetes who have a record of microalbuminuria testing in the previous 15 months (exception reporting for patients with proteinuria).	3	40–90%
DM 22. The percentage of patients with diabetes who have a record of estimated glomerular filtration rate or serum creatinine testing in the previous 15 months.	3	40–90%
DM 15. The percentage of patients with diabetes with proteinuria or microalbuminuria who are treated with ACE inhibitors (or A2 antagonists).	3	40–80%

Table 2. Continued

Diabetes mellitus (diabetes)
This set of indicators refers to patients with both type 1 and type 2 diabetes

Indicator	Points	Payment stages
DM 16. The percentage of patients with diabetes who have a record of total cholesterol in the previous 15 months.	3	40–90%
DM 17. The percentage of patients with diabetes whose last measured total cholesterol within previous 15 months is 5 mmol/L or less.	6	40–70%
DM 18. The percentage of patients with diabetes who have had influenza immunisation in the preceding 1 September to 31 March.	3	40–85%

Table 3. Diagnostic values for diabetes using the oral glucose tolerance test.

	Glucose concentration (mmol/L)			
	Whole blood		Plasma	
	Venous	Capillary	Venous	Capillary
Diabetes mellitus				
Fasting value or	≥6.7	≥6.7	≥7.8	≥7.8
2 hours after glucose load	≥10.0	≥11.1	≥11.1	≥12.2
Impaired glucose tolerance				
Fasting value and	<6.7	<6.7	<7.8	<7.8
2 hours after glucose load	6.7–10.0	7.8–11.1	7.8–11.1	8.9–12.2

Note: for epidemiological or population screening purposes the 2-hour value after administering 75 g oral glucose may be used alone. The fasting value alone is considered to be less reliable since true fasting cannot be assured and the spurious diagnosis of diabetes may more readily occur.

Smoking status and advice

Smoking is an established risk factor for CVD and other diseases. Achieving smoking cessation in people with diabetes is the single most important risk reduction factor. From April 2006, all smoking and smoking cessation indicators in the diabetes domain (and the CHD, stroke, hypertension, COPD and asthma domains) will be removed from the disease indicator sets and placed within two specific smoking indicators worth a total of 68 points.

Glycaemic control

A total of 31 quality points are available in the GMS contract for glycaemic control. There are three points for a record of HbA_{1C} in the previous 15 months. There are two tiers of glycaemic control for which points are awarded. The first, for 17 points, is the percentage of patients for whom the last HbA_{1C} is 7.5% or less. It is important to note the range of payment stages associated with this indicator (40–50%). This means that full points will be awarded if 50% of your patients are below this level. This is just as well, as studies in this country and others show that the average percentage of patients achieving the target HbA_{1C} of 7.0% is about 45%. The contract has some built-in leeway. In recognition of the fact that these levels are difficult to achieve, there is a second tier with an upper limit of HbA_{1C} of 10% and a range of 40–90%. Most practices should be able to achieve these levels. There are a variety of agents available to us in our battle for improved glycaemic control and there are some guiding principles as to which agent should be selected under certain circumstances.

- For most patients requiring oral hypoglycaemic agents, metformin is usually the first drug of choice, particularly if the BMI is over 25. It is important to recognise that some ethnic minorities, especially Asians, have a high prevalence of insulin resistance and central obesity despite a low BMI. In these individuals, it may be appropriate to start metformin if the BMI is over 22.
- If HbA_{1C} levels remain above 7.0%, despite maximum tolerated doses of metformin, then *early* combination therapy will be required, using a sulphonylurea, a postprandial glucose regulator or a glitazone as appropriate and according to tolerability.
- Similarly, if oral therapies are failing, the *early* introduction of insulin, alone or in combination with metformin, should be considered. In the past, there has perhaps been a reluctance *on the part of the healthcare professional* to suggest this direction, reserving it as 'the last resort'. Thankfully, attitudes are changing, and patients are able to benefit from improved glycaemic control and improved well-being. Newer insulins have helped to simplify regimens and reduce episodes of hypoglycaemia.

Retinal screening

There are five quality points available for a record that patients have had retinal screening by an approved retinal screening service within the previous 15 months. This may be by digital photography, or through an optometrist-led service. It is, once again, important to be able to extract this data from source – this may mean liaising with optometrists to obtain a report of findings rather than depending on the patient to report that they 'have had their eyes checked'.

Foot care

When it comes to foot care a total of six quality points are available – three for recording peripheral pulses and three for neuropathy testing. New Read codes have been introduced to enable us to more clearly record these findings. Most patients with diabetes will benefit from a referral to a specialist diabetic chiropody service, but it is important to liaise with these services to enable recording of the all-important data.

Blood pressure control

Second only to glycaemic control as a 'point grabber' with a total of 21 points, three for a record of blood pressure in the past 15 months and 18 points for attaining levels of 145/85 mmHg in 60% of patients. UKPDS showed that tight control of blood pressure in type 2 diabetes is central to cardiovascular risk reduction, furthermore any reduction in blood pressure confers a lower risk of developing complications. If lifestyle changes do not reduce blood pressure levels to target levels, antihypertensive agents need to be considered. There is no optimal recommended first-line antihypertensive agent, but in patients with microalbuminuria, an ACE inhibitor or an angiotensin II receptor blocker should be used. Again, *early* combination therapy to achieve target levels should be considered. Until new guidance is issued, it seems appropriate to follow the latest BHS guidelines regarding the choice of antihypertensive. Many patients will end up on three or more agents, but as blood pressure control was shown to be more effective than glycaemic control in reducing complications in the UKPDS, and as hypertension is present in as many as 70% of type 2 diabetics, this is cost-effective treatment, even though it does add to the burden of polypharmacy in our patients.

> Tight control of blood pressure in type 2 diabetes is central to cardiovascular risk reduction.

Renal function

There are nine points available in this category, and it is the area where most practitioners may have the most difficulties. The breakdown is simple enough:
- three points for a record of estimated glomerular filtration rate or serum creatinine
- three points for a record of microalbuminuria testing

- three points for using an ACE inhibitor or an angiotensin II receptor blocker in appropriate cases.

Measuring serum creatinine should prove to have few problems. NICE recommends that patients with type 2 diabetes should have annual microalbuminuria testing. If this is positive, it should be repeated twice; if it remains positive, an ACE inhibitor should be started with regular monitoring of creatinine and electrolyte levels. However, there are logistical problems:

- the test–retest reliability of stick tests is poor
- there are many reasons for a positive reading, necessitating further investigation
- the definitive test is timed urine collection
- some people would argue that the test is irrelevant in the presence of existing CVD, as risk factors are already being addressed
- some people suggest that it is of limited value in the over-70 population.

Perhaps it is for these reasons that repeated surveys and audits show that microalbuminuria testing is the lowest ranking indicator in diabetes care. This is despite the fact that ACE inhibitors and angiotensin II receptor blockers have been shown to reduce progression to renal failure, following early detection of microalbuminuria, and that it represents an independent risk factor for CVD. Thus, more work needs to be done to clarify this situation. Many laboratories will start to report estimated glomerular filtration rates in the near future, with appropriate referral algorithms.

Lipid management

Three points are given for a record of total cholesterol, and a further six points for achieving a value of 5 mmol/L or less. The evidence base for lipid management in diabetes is complex and somewhat overwhelming, with claim and counter-claim appearing almost weekly. Some would advocate a 'statins for all' policy, others prefer individual risk assessment. However, claims are made that the Framingham tables do not apply to diabetes (and indeed there were only about 300 diabetics in the Framingham study), and the more recent HPS and CARDS studies have raised further questions about intervention levels. A simple, but often effective primary care strategy is as follows.

- Secondary prevention: put all patients on a statin.
- Primary prevention: if the total cholesterol is above 5 mmol/L, put them on a statin.

Targets for individual lipid subfractions are also important, so a statin is useful if these levels are out of target range. Of course, it is worth arguing that there is no such thing as primary prevention in type 2 diabetes, as this group has the *same risk of having a major cardiac event as someone without diabetes who has already had an MI.* New advice from the JBS resets intervention levels found within the GMS contract to new targets:

- total cholesterol <4 mmol/L
- LDL-C <2 mmol/L
- triglycerides <1.7 mmol/L.

Influenza immunisation

Finally, three points are awarded for following the advice of the Joint Committee on Vaccination and Immunisation with respect to 'flu jabs.

Conclusions

This ten-point plan unifies existing management guidelines and strategies. Closer inspection, however, reveals that there is nothing new in this plan, and in fact you would probably have checked all the above elements in an annual review (with the exception of thyroid function, which is curiously missing from the quality indicators). The differences are that our performance is now related to pay, and that data collection *and recording from whatever source*, be it primary or secondary care, will be necessary to demonstrate that you have done what you said you would do (and should do!).

Routine blood testing in other clinics frequently throws up results which place patients in the range for impaired fasting glycaemia (i.e. 6.0–6.9mmol/L). There is increasing evidence that targeting individuals with states of impaired glucose metabolism may be beneficial. These groups have a higher risk of progressing to type 2 diabetes and also have an increased cardiovascular risk. Lifestyle intervention in the form of weight management, increased exercise and dietary change has been shown to reduce the risk of progression to type 2 diabetes by as much as 58%. Thus, it would be a good idea to keep a 'subregister' of these individuals to assess the effect of any interventions on their progress.

Targeting individuals with impaired glucose metabolism may be beneficial. These groups have a higher risk of progressing to type 2 diabetes and also have an increased cardiovascular risk.

3. Cardiometabolic disease – a primary care perspective

Managing cardiometabolic risk in practice

This is an opportune time to review the management of patients with cardiometabolic risk, following the recent publication of the Joint British Societies' (JBS) guidelines on the prevention of cardiovascular disease (CVD) in clinical practice.[1]

Cardiometabolic disease comprises CVD (i.e. coronary heart disease [CHD], stroke and transient ischaemic attack [TIA]), diabetes, dyslipidaemia, hypertension and obesity. The increasing prevalence of cardiometabolic disease within the population means that primary care practices need to become as efficient and effective as possible when managing these diseases. One way of optimising resource use in practice is to manage this group of diseases as a single entity (i.e. cardiometabolic disease) rather than as individual diseases *per se*. The clustering and overlap of cardiometabolic risk factors and diseases in individuals and the availability of appropriate interventions which target more than one risk factor, facilitate this process.

The clustering of cardiometabolic risk factors in individuals can be exploited to:

- aid in identifying previously unrecognised high-risk patients
- streamline investigations for newly diagnosed patients
- maximise the benefits of lifestyle interventions
- optimise the use of primary care appointments for global cardiometabolic assessments.

In this very practical section, we will explore ways in which we can optimise our approach to identification, investigation, management and follow-up of these high-risk individuals.

> One way of optimising resource use is to manage this group of diseases as a single entity (i.e. cardiometabolic disease) rather than as individual diseases.

Background to cardiometabolic disease management

There are two distinct populations of patients that fall under the umbrella of cardiometabolic disease.

- Asymptomatic individuals at high risk of developing CVD and diabetes due to a combination of cardiometabolic risk factors – the primary prevention group.
- Individuals who already have CVD and/or diabetes – the secondary prevention group.

Enhanced use of information technology (IT) in primary care since the advent of the new General Medical Services (GMS) contract has greatly facilitated the production of disease registers and also the monitoring and audit of care for patients with chronic disease. These factors have simplified the delivery of good quality care.

Although most practices run CHD and diabetes clinics, forward-looking practices are recognising the practical benefits of combining these and other areas of chronic disease management, such as stroke and hypertension monitoring, into a single cardiometabolic clinic (see Box 1). Experienced primary care professionals also know that an opportunistic approach may be more effective for primary prevention, targeting patients when they first present for consultation, investigating them to identify all cardiometabolic risk factors and encouraging further consultation or attendance at clinics for further treatment and follow-up.

Workload and a lack of resources are important issues facing healthcare professionals. However, the clustering of cardiometabolic diseases and cardiometabolic risk factors means that whilst we have large numbers of patients on our CHD, diabetes, stroke and obesity disease registers, many patients will appear on more than one register. Therefore, these patients can be tackled in a single encounter. This lessens our workload which is further reduced by the effort that the practice teams have already invested in order to meet the GMS Quality and Outcome Framework (QOF), resulting in many patients with CHD, stroke and diabetes already being treated to target.

> Forward-looking practices are recognising the practical benefits of combining CHD, diabetes and other areas of chronic disease management into a single cardiometabolic clinic.

Cardiovascular risk calculators and guidelines

Information on the contribution of the various risk factors that predispose individuals to CVD has come largely from the Framingham Heart Study – a large cohort study which followed people without CVD at recruitment.[2] Data from this study have been used to create risk factor tables, which allow calculation of an individual's 10-year risk of CHD and CVD. However, it is important to note that Framingham scores can underestimate the magnitude of risk in individuals with insulin resistance or diabetes.

Box 1. Practical experience of running a cardiometabolic clinic.

The team in Pontardawe Health Centre, Swansea, have been running a very successful nurse-led chronic disease management clinic for some time. Patients with more than one chronic disease attend a special clinic for an annual review appointment in the month of their birthday. This makes it easier for patients to remember to book their appointment and spreads clinic numbers evenly throughout the year. Carrying out all the necessary checks in a single appointment saves time for patients and frees up nurse time for working with patients who need more help to improve disease control.

The Framingham score can be calculated using a computer programme (*cvrisk.mvm.ed.ac.uk/calculator.htm*) or read off graphs published in the *British National Formulary* (*www.bnf.org.uk*).

The new JBS guidelines published in 2005 make recommendations on how to use the current risk calculator to estimate 10-year CVD risk in individual patients.[1] These recommendations are summarised in Box 2. For the first time these guidelines recommend giving equal priority to managing all those at high risk, including:

- those with established CVD
- those with diabetes
- asymptomatic individuals without CVD but whose 10-year CVD risk is 20% or greater.

In addition, those with single risk factors such as hypertension, a ratio of total cholesterol (TC) to high density lipoprotein cholesterol (HDL-C) of six or higher, or familial dyslipidaemia need appropriate treatment to lower their risk of CVD (Box 2).

Practicalities of disease management

This section highlights a few aspects of identification, investigation, management and follow-up, and makes some suggestions for practical ways to achieve these tasks more efficiently and effectively. A key theme is how we deal with the different cardiometabolic risk factors and diseases as a group, rather than looking at them as separate entities, thus making the most of the synergy that is possible.

Efficiencies can be achieved by:

- avoiding duplicate appointments for individual patients
- ensuring clear goals both for the primary care team and for patients
- agreeing and utilising stepwise protocols to treat to targets
- using computer templates to ensure accurate data collection and collation
- using IT systems to prepare reports and opportunistically 'flag-up' patients with missing data
- optimising patient empowerment and encouraging individuals to take increased responsibility for their own health
- targeting therapy appropriately.

Identification of high-risk groups

Established cardiometabolic disease – the secondary prevention population

The QOF has ensured that most practices are now computerised and that accurate disease registers for CVD (i.e. CHD, stroke and TIA) and diabetes are now available. Patients on these registers need immediate management and, consequently, there is no need to calculate their CVD

Box 2. Calculating cardiovascular disease (CVD) risk.[1] Risk assessment charts are printed at the back of the *British National Formulary*.

- Determine the individual's age, gender, smoking status, systolic blood pressure, non-fasting TC and HDL-C and non-fasting glucose; calculate the TC/HDL-C ratio.

- Use the appropriate graph or online calculator (*cvrisk.mvm.ed.ac.uk/calculator.htm*) to estimate the individual's 10-year CVD risk.

- Take into account the individual's ethnicity, family history of CVD, obesity, central obesity, elevated triglycerides, impaired glucose regulation or target organ damage. Subjectively revise CVD risk accordingly.

Notes

- Consider the individual's lifetime smoking habit not just their current status; estimate the lifetime exposure in pack years; consider the time elapsed since quitting.

- Use an average of two systolic blood pressure readings.

- Use a random glucose sample if it is below 6.0 mmol/L, but repeat fasting glucose test if it is 6.1 mmol/L and above.

- Use pre-treatment systolic blood pressure and lipid levels if the individual is already receiving treatment. If these values are not available then assume a systolic blood pressure of 160 mmHg and a TC/HDL-C ratio of 6.

- Initiate lipid-lowering therapy (or continue therapy) even if modification of risk factors (e.g. hypertension treatment) results in the calculated risk falling below the treatment threshold.

- If lifestyle advice results in blood pressure or lipid levels falling below treatment targets, don't treat, but re-evaluate annually.

Certain groups are considered high risk and should receive appropriate treatment without the need for a risk calculation. Those with:

- CVD

- blood pressure ≥160/100 mmHg or evidence of target organ damage

- TC/HDL ratio ≥6

- diabetes

- renal dysfunction

- familial hyperlipidaemias.

HDL-C, high density lipoprotein cholesterol; LDL-C, low density lipoprotein cholesterol; TC, total cholesterol.

risk.[1] Data quality reviews, for example identifying those patients who are currently receiving diuretics and/or aspirin and checking whether they are included on the appropriate disease register, will identify those who were previously diagnosed but missing from registers. Opportunistic urinalysis or blood pressure checks will uncover the truly undiagnosed patients.

High cardiometabolic risk group – the primary prevention population

The new JBS guidelines recommend that individuals whose total 10-year CVD risk is 20% or higher should be identified and treated as aggressively as those with established CVD or diabetes.[1] Practices are becoming increasingly effective at identifying these patients opportunistically. However, very few practices will have screened all their patients over the age of 40 years in an effort to assess 10-year CVD risk – as is now recommended in the JBS 2 guidelines – let alone offering such assessment to younger patients who have a family history of early onset CVD.[1]

Individuals with a single cardiometabolic risk factor require treatment even if they do not meet the total 10-year CVD risk of 20% or greater.[1] These cardiometabolic risk factors include:

- a systolic blood pressure of 160 mmHg or higher or a diastolic blood pressure of 100 mmHg or higher (lower targets apply for patients with target organ damage and these are stratified by the GMS contract to 90 mmHg diastolic for hypertension and 85 mmHg for those with diabetes)
- a TC/HDL-C ratio of six or higher
- familial hyperlipidaemia.

The new JBS guidelines recommend that individuals whose total 10-year CVD risk is 20% or higher should be identified and treated as aggressively as those with established CVD or diabetes.

Practice register of patients with obesity

From 2006 practices will be rewarded for developing an obesity register (with obesity defined as a body mass index [BMI] of ≥ 30). Rather than simply measuring an individual's BMI, this development offers practices an ideal opportunity to also record waist circumference, which is a valuable surrogate marker for visceral fat and central obesity. Central obesity (defined as waist circumference of 94 cm or higher for Europid men and 80 cm or higher for Europid women) predicts increased cardiometabolic risk more accurately than high BMI.

If the practice has a low level of baseline BMI recording, then 'eyeballing' patients to decide who should be formally weighed and measured will ensure that the obesity register is achieved as rapidly as possible. Scales and Post-it® notes in a screened area of the waiting room may encourage self-weighing whilst waiting, or positioning the scales where patients can step on and off easily on the way out of the consulting room can facilitate data collection.

Tape measures showing the increased risk zones for waist circumference ('Waist Watchers' tape measures) are available from pharmaceutical companies and are motivational. When measuring waist circumference always measure either the narrowest circumference between the ribs and the pelvis, or at a level midway between the rib cage and pelvic brim at the end of full expiration. For consistency across the register, also ensure your whole team use the same measurement method. Many authorities recommend that a waist-to-hip ratio is recorded. The hips are measured at their widest point. The waist-to-hip ratio should be 0.90 or lower in men or 0.83 or lower in women.

Since most obese patients will have additional cardiometabolic risk factors, practices need to agree on how to collect the additional data from those identified as obese.

Although all computer systems calculate BMI, most do not currently allow numerical waist circumference recording so you will need to amend the codes to allow for this. Incorporating these codes into health templates will facilitate data collection.

Since most obese patients will have additional cardiometabolic risk factors, practices need to agree on how to collect the additional data from those identified as obese. Some consultations will allow the completion of a full health template. On other occasions, a separate consultation will be needed for further data collection, further investigation and lifestyle counselling.

Finding new patients with diabetes and hypertension

Most practices are already actively searching for cases of undiagnosed diabetes. The association between cardiometabolic risk factors means that patients with obesity are more likely to have dyslipidaemia, diabetes and hypertension. Therefore, screening people with a BMI of 30 or higher or those with a high waist circumference (i.e. ≥94 cm for Europid men and ≥80 cm for Europid women) for diabetes and impaired glucose tolerance will provide a higher return than screening all individuals aged over 40 years. Identifying these individuals may also help us to prevent patients progressing to diabetes and CVD. Similarly, most practices have only 50% of their hypertensive patients diagnosed. Targeting blood pressure checks to the obese is also likely to have a higher pick-up rate than screening a random selection of patients.

Identifying other high-risk patients

The clustering of cardiometabolic risk factors in high-risk individuals means that the identification of one risk factor should prompt a search for other risk factors. For example, diagnosing hypertension should prompt not only investigations for hypertension but also blood glucose, lipid profile, BMI and waist circumference measurements, together with collection of family history and lifestyle information, if this has not been performed previously.

Patient self-measurement and information gathering

Questionnaires can be used with existing patients to update risk factor information either opportunistically, when they attend surgery, or by post.

Many practices encourage patients to measure blood pressure and weight in screened parts of the waiting area and then discuss and code these measurements during the consultation. Cardiometabolic family history, past medical history and smoking history feature heavily in new patient questionnaires. These questionnaires can also be used with existing patients to update risk factor information either opportunistically, when they attend surgery, or by post.

Using the metabolic syndrome to identify high-risk groups

If waist circumference is recorded in health templates, and we apply the International Diabetes Federation (IDF) definition of the metabolic syndrome (see Chapter 1), it is possible for some individuals with the metabolic syndrome to be identified via a computer search, thereby allowing intensive risk reduction in these patients. Those with a large waist circumference but who do not meet other criteria for the metabolic syndrome are at lower risk. Those who meet the waist circumference target but have not had other investigations to confirm or refute a diagnosis of the metabolic syndrome can be targeted for further assessment. Again, this is a fertile ground for identifying new cases of diabetes.

Investigation

One question, three measurements and three investigations for cardiometabolic assessment

Although it is challenging treating to the targets of the QOF, cardiometabolic risk assessment involves only one question, three measurements and three investigations, with seven other investigations for specific patients with established disease.

- Ask about smoking.
- Measure height, weight and blood pressure.
- Check fasting lipid profile, blood glucose (for screening) or glycated haemoglobin (HbA_{1C}) (for patients with established diabetes) and creatinine.

    Performing all of these at once is more efficient (for both the patient and the healthcare team) than, for example, checking fasting lipids because the patient is obese but later realising that their blood pressure is high necessitating a creatinine level. Patients with newly diagnosed angina may need an exercise stress test; new stroke or TIA patients will need a computed tomography (CT) scan and carotid Doppler scanning and patients with diabetes will need retinal screening, foot pulses, neuropathy testing and microalbuminuria checks.

Management

Delivering lifestyle advice

All patients with cardiometabolic risk factors need lifestyle advice, ideally from a dietitian and exercise professional, and follow-up to motivate them to comply with this advice. Since the same lifestyle interventions are effective for all cardiometabolic risks, this simplifies advice and allows streamlining of information provision.

All patients with cardiometabolic risk factors need lifestyle advice, ideally from a dietitian and exercise professional, and follow-up to motivate them to comply with this advice.

In reality, however, very few practices have the benefit of dietetic advice during all clinics. Therefore, it is important to work with the dietitian and exercise professionals to prepare information materials to use for patients, or agree high quality ready-made resources to use.

The typical Mediterranean diet (i.e. a diet rich in fruit and vegetables, olive oil and oily fish, and low in saturated fat) appears to reduce all of the established cardiometabolic risk factors, and is relatively easy to describe to patients. In general, it is best to aim for less than 30% of total calorific intake to be derived from fat. Encouraging the patient to replace highly processed foods with fresh foods is also a good starting point and keeps the messages simple.

Walking is the best exercise to recommend and is usually safe even in high-risk groups. Many primary care organisations (PCOs) now provide pedometers (or these can be bought relatively cheaply) and these can encourage patients to gradually increase activity levels. For example, encourage patients to start from their current step count and make weekly 10% increments thereafter until they achieve the goal of 10,000 steps daily. Many practices can now refer patients with cardiometabolic risk factors to 'Exercise on referral' schemes where qualified instructors prepare personalised exercise programmes incorporating aerobic and resistance exercise. Such schemes encourage long-term participation in physical activity and adoption of healthy lifestyles.

Many practices can now refer patients with cardiometabolic risk factors to 'Exercise on referral' schemes. Such schemes encourage long-term participation in physical activity and adoption of healthy lifestyles.

Readiness to change and lifestyle counselling

Encouraging patients to adopt healthier lifestyles in an effort to reduce their cardiometabolic risk can be very challenging, particularly in the limited time that is available during a routine consultation in primary care. In Box 3, Professor Christopher Butler discusses various methods by which clinicians can identify patients' attitude towards lifestyle change and how they can tailor their interviewing and counselling skills in an effort to achieve an efficient outcome for all parties concerned.

Smoking: reduce then quit

All smokers should be encouraged to quit. Nicotine replacement and oral therapies such as bupropion increase quit rates. Currently patients are encouraged to reduce their daily cigarette count before finally setting a date to quit. Most primary care teams now have access to smoking cessation services. Referring those patients who are ready to change (Box 3) will save practice staff time for other tasks that cannot currently be outsourced.

Clear goal setting for patients

Agreeing clear goals with patients before embarking on lifestyle counselling or drug therapy may increase their concordance or persistence with therapy. Charts or cards that record the goals negotiated and agreed with

Box 3. Promoting behaviour change to reduce cardiometabolic risk.

Professor Christopher Butler

In the traditional 'medical model' consultation, patients present problems to clinicians who ask a series of (usually) closed questions, order tests, make a diagnosis and then decide upon best management. Here, the clinician is acting like a 'director', in charge and making decisions. Although this 'directive' style of consultation can be highly appropriate (e.g. in acute emergencies), problems arise when it is applied to anticipatory and chronic care situations.

Health-threatening behaviours account for up to 40% of all annual total deaths and 70% of all healthcare expenditure in the Western world. Simply telling people who engage in such behaviours what they need to do to reduce these risks has not worked. But why not?

Research from the field of psychology and addiction suggests that people are more likely to change if decisions are 'owned' rather than imposed on them from the outside. This is particularly true when lifelong change is being considered, since this has to be implemented by patients and needs to fit into their complex lives. Early research in the field of motivational interviewing showed that the more clinicians argued with patients and confronted and cajoled them to change, the less likely the patients were to change.

The role of the clinician in the field of behavioural change may therefore more usefully be conceived of as a 'guide' rather than as a 'director'. A good guide is someone with a lot of useful experience and information who finds out:

- what the goals of the patient are
- where they want to go
- what mode will suit them best in trying to get there
- what support they need.

Information gleaned from the patient is supplemented with ideas and support from the guide. This relationship can be genuinely considered a 'meeting of experts', with the patient expert in how they feel about things and what may and may not work in the context of their own lives, and the clinician expert in providing the structure for eliciting these things from the patient, enhancing the motivation of the patient and providing expertise particularly on content about the 'why' and 'how' of change.

This raises the practicalities of clinical method. How does a clinician become a successful 'guide'? In order to change, people must generally be convinced that change is important (the 'why' of change) and that they can successfully implement change (the 'how' of change). In any given group, there is generally great variation along these two dimensions. Some are not yet convinced that they should change whilst others are literally 'dying' to change but just can't manage it. To be effective and efficient, clinicians need to interact very differently according to where an individual patient is regarding the 'why' and 'how' of change (Figure 1).

After establishing a rapport with patients, clinicians may wish to determine whether the patient is struggling mainly with the 'why' of change or the 'how' of change. If it is the former, then attempting to enhance the importance of change is a useful target. Try asking such a patient to reflect on the 'pros and cons' from their point of view of the behaviour under discussion (Figure 1). With this 'pros and cons strategy', the clinician first asks the patient what they like or enjoy about their behaviour, then asks them what they dislike about it, and then crucially, the clinician asks the patient to reflect on the balance they have set up. If the problem is more one of 'how to change' then an option is to 'brainstorm solutions' with the patient, where the clinician-guide first asks the patient to make suggestions about what they have tried previously or what may work for them now (Figure 1). The clinician then supplements this with additional ideas and then the patient is invited to choose a feasible option for themselves. Notice in both the 'pros and cons' and 'brainstorming solutions' strategies, the patient remains an active participant throughout,

Box 3. Continued

'working hard' to bring their 'expertise' to bear in the consultation. Ultimately, their input helps set up decisions and they are then invited to make and take responsibility for the decisions.

This moves the consultation on from the 'directive' medical model approach to seeing the clinician as far more than a 'disease management expert'. The clinician becomes an expert in eliciting and enhancing patients' motivation to change and working with them to identify practical options for change and supporting them in this.

In this 'guiding' model, clinicians need to be expert at asking questions and providing information in ways that are efficient and useful. One key to doing this successfully is to ensure that clinicians skilfully balance 'instructing', 'asking' and 'listening'. It can be revealing to consider how much time in the consultation is taken up with 'instructing' and whether this information is meeting the patient's information needs? So 'ask' what the patient already knows and what they would like to know. In this way, one avoids wasting time telling people what may be already well known (for example, 'smoking is bad for your health'). Ask what information they would like to receive. Is the pace about right for them? Have they heard what you have been saying? And crucially, always ask what the patient makes of it; what does it mean to them in their current situation? In this way, the limited time that can be devoted to behaviour change will be well targeted. Instead of patients waiting for the ritual lecture about well-known threats to be over when a guiding style is used, patients are generally sitting forward in their seats with an engaged expression, talking as much, or even more than the clinician, and reflecting hard on 'why' they might change and 'how' they can achieve that change.

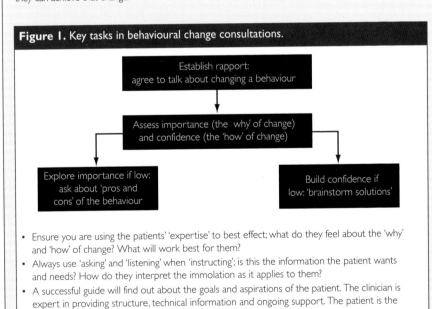

Figure 1. Key tasks in behavioural change consultations.

Establish rapport: agree to talk about changing a behaviour

Assess importance (the 'why' of change) and confidence (the 'how' of change)

Explore importance if low: ask about 'pros and cons' of the behaviour

Build confidence if low: 'brainstorm solutions'

- Ensure you are using the patients' 'expertise' to best effect; what do they feel about the 'why' and 'how' of change? What will work best for them?
- Always use 'asking' and 'listening' when 'instructing'; is this the information the patient wants and needs? How do they interpret the immolation as it applies to them?
- A successful guide will find out about the goals and aspirations of the patient. The clinician is expert in providing structure, technical information and ongoing support. The patient is the expert decision maker about their life, their goals, and what is feasible for them.

patients can be motivational and remind both them and us what we were aiming for when they attend for review. Space on the reverse for recording measurements and progress is also useful. An example of such a chart is shown in Box 4. Patient organisations, pharmaceutical companies and nutraceutical companies can provide these charts.

Working with external agencies

Many practices do not have the resources to provide diet or exercise advice to their patients or to motivate them to make appropriate lifestyle changes. 'Weight Watchers', 'Slimming World' and other patient groups provide sensible diet and lifestyle advice combined with peer-group support and motivation. Although historically there has been a reluctance to recommend these to patients, in the real world, participation in these groups can greatly improve the chances of patients taking action.

Protocol-driven management plans for the team

Most practices already have protocols in place for the management of chronic diseases, including clear treatment targets. Protocols for obesity and dyslipidaemia may also be needed. An A4-laminated card with all the treatment targets agreed by the practice (whether or not these match those set out in the QOF) will allow the rapid assessment of the need for therapy changes during patient review. If you already have all the necessary protocols and are happy with them, simply ensure that they are updated when new targets are set, for example on publication of new guidelines or QOF targets.

Follow-up and adherence with therapy

De-duplicating clinic attendance

Although it is important to maintain separate registers for the different QOF domains, de-duplication of registers will allow us to identify the overlap between the patient groups when scheduling reviews. When patients attend they can then have two or more templates completed.

For example, all practices already have disease registers for CHD (G3%), diabetes (C10%) and hypertension (G20%). Computer searches will identify overlaps between different groups and demonstrate how many clinic appointments could be saved if each patient attended a cardiometabolic clinic rather than once for each review (Box 5). When patients attend for review, the computer flags up which templates need completion.

Computer searches will identify overlaps between different groups and demonstrate how many clinic appointments could be saved if each patient attended a cardiometabolic clinic rather than once for each review.

GMS contract targets and beyond

Many practices are achieving all the QOF targets and may choose to implement the lower blood pressure and lipid targets currently recommended in the JBS 2 guidelines (Box 6). Alternatively, they may

Box 4. An example of a patient goal chart for cardiometabolic risk factors.

Cardiometabolic risk factor	Goal	Management options	Starting point	Interim goal
Blood pressure	Non-diabetic <150/90 mmHg Diabetic <145/85 mmHg	Decrease salt intake Eat five portions of fruit and vegetables a day Walk five times per week Drug treatment		
Total cholesterol	≤5 mmol/L	Mediterranean diet Benecol® or Flora Proactiv® Soya products Increase activity levels Drug treatment		
BMI	<25	Mediterranean diet Increase activity levels Use pedometer Build up to walk briskly 30 minutes five times per week Drug treatments (only if weight loss achieved with lifestyle changes)		Lose 5 kg Lose 10 kg BMI <30
Waist circumference	Male ≤94 cm Female ≤80 cm	Mediterranean diet Increase activity levels Use pedometer Build up to walk briskly 30 minutes five times per week Drug treatment (only if weight loss achieved with lifestyle changes)		Male ≤102 cm Female ≤88cm
HbA$_{1C}$	<7%	Mediterranean diet Increase activity levels Use pedometer Build up to walk briskly 30 minutes five times per week Drug treatment		1% below current level
Smoking	Non-smoker	Smoking cessation clinic Nicotine replacement therapy		Reduce the number of cigarettes smoked per day Set quit date

BMI, body mass index; HbA$_{1C}$, glycated haemoglobin.

Box 5. Appointment savings through establishing cardiometabolic disease clinics.

Grove Medical Centre, Swansea

List size: 6,929
CHD register: 253 (4%)
DM register: 229 (3%)
Hypertension register: 748 (11%)
Total appointments needed for single disease annual reviews: 1,230

CHD, DM, hypertension – 33 patients: **saves 66 appointments**
CHD and DM only – 54 patients minus 33 above: **saves 21 appointments**
CHD and hypertension only – 116 patients minus 33: **saves 83 appointments**
DM and hypertension only – 124 patients minus 33: **saves 91 appointments**

Potential total saving: **261 appointments (>20%)**

CHD, coronary heart disease; DM, diabetes mellitus.

Box 6. Quality outcomes framework (QOF) versus Joint British Societies (JBS) treatment targets.

Risk factor	QOF target	JBS target
Systolic blood pressure	≤150 mmHg	<140 mmHg
	≤145 mmHg for DM	<130 mmHg for CHD, DM or CRF
Diastolic blood pressure	≤90 mmHg	<85 mmHg
	≤85 mmHg for DM	<80 mmHg for CHD, DM and CRF
Total cholesterol	<5 mmol/L	<4 mmol/L or a 25% reduction, whichever lower
LDL-C	No target	<2 mmol/L or a 30% reduction, whichever lower
Diabetic control (HbA$_{1C}$)	<7%	≤6.5%

CHD, coronary heart disease; CRF, chronic renal failure; DM, diabetes mellitus; HbA$_{1C}$, glycated haemoglobin; LDL-C, low density lipoprotein cholesterol.

---

wish to embark on identification of previously undiagnosed high-risk patients. This is valuable work as it is anticipated that the QOF will set lower blood pressure and lipid targets in future years. These will take time to achieve, so starting early can only increase future points.

Access data collected in hospital clinics

Many of our highest risk patients are seen regularly in hospital clinics. Hospital staff should be encouraged to share the data they collect thereby allow primary care teams direct access to the results of their investigations. Sharing results also lessens pressure on laboratories, which have been forced to bear the brunt of increased workload resulting from the QOF without any extra funding being made available. PCOs can help in negotiating this.

Motivation and patient empowerment

Helping patients to set clear goals and choose which risk factors they want to target as a priority, should help to improve motivation and patient empowerment. Helping patients understand the role of individual medications and the health benefits of treating to target may improve concordance and persistence with therapies, particularly for asymptomatic conditions. Providing goal cards (Box 4) and including disease information on dosing sections of scripts is easily achieved and may have a significant impact.

Helping patients to set clear goals and choose which risk factors they want to target as a priority, should help improve motivation and patient empowerment.

Case studies

The two case studies illustrated in Boxes 7 and 8 demonstrate the difference between managing individual risk factors as they become clinically apparent compared with opportunistically carrying out a full CVD risk assessment in an obese patient and aggressively managing the risk factors that are identified. Obviously individual patient motivation impacts on the relative outcome. However, these case studies demonstrate that early global reduction in cardiometabolic risk factors reduces long-term CVD risk and can delay or prevent development of diabetes and CVD.

The primary care team and concordance

In the UK the multidisciplinary primary healthcare team work together to diagnose and manage cardiometabolic risk. GPs and practice nurses are ideally placed to identify those at highest risk of CVD and diabetes within the practice setting.

GPs and practice nurses are ideally placed to identify those at highest risk of CVD and diabetes within the practice setting.

In some PCOs, GPs with Special Interest (GPwSIs) are providing community-based cardiology or diabetes services and may use their expertise to deliver services, help educate primary care teams, or work to modify the structure of the service provision in their area.

Encouraging patient concordance, that is, adherence to the regimen of care recommended by the doctor, has been a common problem for the primary care team for a long time.[3] Only about 50% of people with chronic disease comply with their doctor's recommendations, irrespective of the nature of the disease, its treatment or the patient's age. For example, in those with treated hypertension, 50% will stop taking their drugs during the first year of treatment. This means that patients who have been diagnosed with the cardiometabolic syndrome should be encouraged to set their own therapeutic goals and be encouraged to adhere to their medication at follow up. The primary care team

> **Box 7.** Case study one.
>
> Norman is 37 years old. He presents with back pain and is found to have elevated blood pressure when this is measured opportunistically. Repeat measurements demonstrate levels that are persistently above 170/100 mmHg.
>
> **Additional data collected**
> - Height 1.77 m
> - Weight 112.7 kg
> - BMI 35.6
> - Waist circumference 130 cm
> - Fundoscopy normal
> - Urea, electrolytes, creatinine normal
> - ECG normal
> - Family history of diabetes and CHD
>
> Despite lifestyle advice to stop smoking, increase exercise, lose weight and reduce salt intake, his blood pressure remains around 168/98 and so he is initiated on an ACE inhibitor.
>
> One year later he presents with thirst and polyuria, and urinalysis shows +++ of glucose. Fasting glucose levels are 8.6 and 9.3, confirming diabetes. Blood pressure is 150/88 mmHg. However, with the diagnosis of diabetes, a lower blood pressure target of <145/85 mmHg is agreed, and a calcium-channel blocker is added. Despite dietary and lifestyle advice, his HbA_{1C} remains high and he is started on metformin, which he tolerates well.
>
> - BMI 34.6
> - Waist circumference 135 cm
> - TC 6.7 mmol/L
> - HDL-C 0.9 mmol/L
> - TC/HDL 7.44
>
> A statin is initiated and the dose increased whilst monitoring his liver function and lipid profile.
>
> He is reviewed 6 monthly in the diabetic clinic and annually in the hypertension clinic. Unfortunately, 2 years after his initial hypertension diagnosis, he suffers a myocardial infarction followed by a small CVA.
>
> ACE, angiotensin-converting enzyme; BMI, body mass index; CVA, cerebrovascular accident; CHD, coronary heart disease; ECG, electrocardiogram; HbA_{1C}, glycated haemoglobin; HDL-C, high density lipoprotein cholesterol; TC, total cholesterol.

encounter such patients regularly for follow-up and contract-related reviews, and are ideally placed to encourage greater adherence.

For therapeutic regimens to be successful the patient's feelings and thoughts about the condition should be fully engaged, they should be made fully aware of the potential of the syndrome to cause long-term harm and encouraged into a concordant relationship with their prescriber to ensure long-term persistence with treatment regimens.

Patient should be encouraged into a concordant relationship with their prescriber to ensure long-term persistence with treatment regimens.

Patient empowerment

Box 8. Case study two.

Norman has a brother Jack who is aged 35 years. He presents to his GP with headache. He smokes 15 cigarettes per day.

On opportunistic examination:
- Height 172.7 cm
- Weight 106.3 Kg
- Waist circumference 110 cm
- BMI 35.6
- Blood pressure 147/92 mmHg

As he has a family history of early onset CVD, is obese, with a waist circumference which puts him at risk of the metabolic syndrome, he is fully investigated and seen in the practice cardiometabolic risk clinic.

- Fasting blood glucose 6.7 mmol/L
- TC 6.3 mmol/L
- HDL-C 0.9 mmol/L
- TC/HDL-C ratio 7.0
- Oral glucose tolerance test – impaired fasting glucose
- Urinalysis normal

Rather than just managing his obesity, performing a full CVD risk assessment in the cardiometabolic risk clinic identified other ways to reduce his overall risk. He was motivated to undertake lifestyle interventions. He stopped smoking and was given diet advice and referred for exercise on prescription. When this failed to reduce his TC/HDL ratio to below 6, he was started on a low-dose statin. Gradually his central obesity improved and his fasting glucose level returned to normal. With the combination of statin and lifestyle measures his lipid profile 1 year later showed:

- TC 4.8
- HDL-C 1.1
- TC/HDL-C ratio 4.36.

Five years later his waist circumference had fallen to 101 cm, his BMI to 29.4, blood pressure to 145/85 mmHg, fasting blood glucose to 4.8 mmol/L, and his lipid profile remained well-controlled on a low-dose statin with no side-effects. He remains a non-smoker.

Patient empowerment depends on three concepts: choices, control and consequences.

The personal choices an individual with the cardiometabolic syndrome makes have the greatest impact on their health and well-being, and can have more impact than the influence of their healthcare professionals. Patients who understand and engage with their condition are likely to make the best choices.

Giving the patient back control in the form of self-management usually improves concordance. People with the cardiometabolic syndrome are in control of their own diet and exercise and can decide whether to take medication that is offered by their prescriber. The person ultimately has to live with the consequences of these choices and enjoy the health

has to live with the consequences of these choices and enjoy the health gain that can be achieved by making the right choices.

To bring about active change, strategic alliances between members of the primary care team, patients and their carers have become increasingly important. By working together and sharing expertise, it is possible to encourage positive change and ultimately participation in treatment plans. People with cardiometabolic conditions will need better information, both for patients about the treatment options available, and for health and social care professionals about what patients need and value.

The future

Metabolic syndrome – does it exist?

The symptom complex of insulin resistance, hyperinsulinaemia, dyslipidaemia, hypertension, hypercoagulability and (central) obesity is widely recognised as the metabolic syndrome. Either insulin resistance or central obesity are thought to be the underlying factors causing the syndrome, which in turn increases the risk of diabetes and CVD.

The IDF criteria for the diagnosis of the metabolic syndrome are reiterated in Box 9. It is important to remember to apply the ethnic origin and not the country of residence of the patient when determining waist circumference.[4]

This new definition has triggered debate, and the American Diabetes Association (ADA) and the European Association for the Study of Diabetes (EASD) recently released a joint statement questioning the existence of the metabolic syndrome (see Chapter 1).[5] However, we do know that people with the metabolic syndrome have a higher total

---

Box 9. The International Diabetes Federation (IDF) diagnostic criteria for the metabolic syndrome.

High waist circumference (see below) plus two of:
- raised blood pressure (≥130/85 mmHg)
- low serum HDL-C (<1.00 mmol/L in men and <1.3 mmol/L in women)
- a high serum triglyceride concentration (≥1.7 mmol/L)
- a high fasting plasma glucose concentration (≥5.6 mmol/L).

IDF waist circumference cut-offs (recognise ethnic variation)

	Men	Women
Europid	≥94 cm (37.0 inches)	≥80 cm (31.5 inches)
South Asian	≥90 cm (35.4 inches)	≥80 cm (31.5 inches)
Chinese	≥90 cm (35.4 inches)	≥80 cm (31.5 inches)
Japanese	≥85 cm (33.5 inches)	≥90 cm (35.4 inches)

but without the syndrome. This risk predictor for increased mortality, the increasing number of people with the condition, the increasing ability to intervene at this stage and the ability to stratify the condition for racial differences makes it a condition which is likely to remain important and relevant for those interested in reducing premature cardiovascular death.

Polypill

A recent article in the *British Medical Journal* proposed the introduction of the polypill.[6] This is a combination of:

- a statin (e.g. low-dose atorvastatin)
- three blood pressure-lowering drugs (e.g. a thiazide diuretic, possibly a β-blocker, and an angiotensin-converting enzyme [ACE] inhibitor), each at half the standard dose
- folic acid (0.8 mg)
- aspirin (75 mg).

The authors estimated that long-term treatment with this combination could reduce CHD events by 88% and stroke by 80%. One-third of people taking this pill from the age of 55 years would benefit and would gain, on average, about 11 years of life free from a CHD event or stroke. It would be acceptably safe and with widespread use could have a greater impact on the prevention of disease in the Western world than any other single intervention.

Polymeal

Although it started off as a humorous suggestion, the concept of using nutrition to reduce CVD risk now has a supportive evidence base. The original proposed diet included wine, fish, dark chocolate, fruits, vegetables, garlic and almonds. Experts suggest that consuming these antioxidant-rich ingredients on a daily basis could reduce cardiovascular disease events by as much as 76%. For men, eating the Polymeal daily could increase life expectancy by 6.6 years and increase life expectancy free from CVD by 9.0 years. Such a meal would neither have the availability nor the applicability of the Polypill, but reminds us there is an alternative to drug treatment for those who are willing to make extensive lifestyle changes. A variety of nutraceuticals such as plant stanols and sterols, soya milk, eggs and milk rich in omega-3 fats and antioxidant/antiplatelet fruit juices make useful additions to the diet and some have been shown to reduce CVD risk factors.

Future NHS changes

In England practices are now being encouraged to engage in the commissioning of care. In Box 10, Professor Mike Kirby outlines the importance and the likely impact of these changes.

Box 10. Implications of practice based commissioning and payment by results for future cardiometabolic risk management

Professor Michael Kirby

The NHS is going through a process of devolving responsibility and accountability to a local level. Payment by Results (PbR), which will lead to an expansion of patient choice, combined with the initiation of Practice Based Commissioning (PBC) will lead to more local control and more local choices. Practices now have the opportunity to group together, not only to take advantage of the levers of PBC to deliver care pathways for their patients, but also as a defence mechanism against the possible threats of the independent sector moving in and bidding for work via the Alternative Provider Medical Services (APMS), which allows private companies or other groups to bid to run primary care services.

The new arrangements will be centred around the patient and quality. The tariff will be set and non-negotiable and therefore the commissioners will make decisions on quality, and better value will come from new pathways and different ways of delivery. This will provide opportunities, which if implemented successfully, will help identify and tackle key local issues and support the delivery of both local and national targets. PbR is a new way of moving funds around the NHS.

Block funding will become a thing of the past and services will be paid for as they are carried out. It means that the provider will get paid for what they have done rather than for what they say they are going to do. PbR will allow duality and enable a number of different providers to come into the system and give patients a choice. Without PbR patient choice would not work because funding would stay with the main trust.

From the providers' point of view they will get fair rewards for the work they do and there will be a degree of transparency about what they are being paid to do. To make this work, NHS trusts will be forced to have sharper budget discipline because they will not be able to overspend since they only get paid for what they have done. They will also be forced to respond to patient choice and preference, in competition with other providers.

Importantly Primary Care Trusts (PCTs) will have to keep their costs within the tariffs and that is a major risk for them. From the point of view of secondary care trusts, careful coding will be essential, ensuring that the trust gets paid for what it has done. There are issues about new developments for providers, which may bring initial costs which are not funded under PbR. From the commissioning body's point of view the level of demand will be critical. They will have to face the full cost of emergency care.

Cardiometabolic risk management will be critically important in preventing both emergency and planned procedures in secondary care. Primary care based interventions are cost effective. Countries with strong primary care systems have lower healthcare costs and healthier populations.[1] The strong performance of practices following the introduction of the 2004 General Medical Services (GMS) contract is something that we should all be very proud of in primary care. The contract invested in evidence-based interventions in primary care and encouraged the further expansion of chronic disease management, including diabetes care, in a practice-based setting.[2] Substantial improvements have been seen in the quality of care for both coronary heart disease and type 2 diabetes[3] and nurse-led secondary prevention clinics for coronary heart disease in primary care have been shown to be very cost effective.[4]

Practice-led primary and secondary prevention will become increasingly important with PbR and PBC. The recent guidelines from the Joint British Societies (JBS) provide a clear lead to facilitate doing the right thing, to the right patient, at the right time and in the right place. Pockets of poor quality are

Box 10. Continued

known to exist, especially in areas of deprivation and for commissioning groups, this will be a major challenge for the future.

References

1 Starfield B. New paradigms for quality in primary care. *Br J Gen Pract* 2001; **51**: 303–9.
2 NHS Confederation. New GMS contract. *www.nhsconfed.org/gms* Accessed 24/01/06.
3 Campbell SM, Roland MO, Middleton E *et al*. Improvements in quality of clinical care in English general practice 1998–2003; longitudinal observational study. *BMJ* 2005; **331**: 1121–3.
4 Rafferty JP, Guiqing LY, Meuchie P *et al*. Cost-effectiveness of nurse-led secondary prevention clinics for coronary heart disease in primary care: follow-up of a randomised controlled trial. *BMJ* 2005; **330**: 707–10.

Conclusions

The cardiometabolic syndrome is becoming increasingly recognised by primary care teams who wish to extend their care from being reactive to patient illness, to proactive in attempting to reduce the considerable morbidity and mortality which follows in the wake of this defined syndrome. A complex but effective series of interventions, both lifestyle and pharmaceutical, will help empower patients with this syndrome to manage their condition successfully.

References

1 British Cardiac Society, British Hypertension Society, Diabetes UK, HEART UK, Primary Care Cardiovascular Society, The Stroke Association. JBS 2: Joint British Societies' guidelines on prevention of cardiovascular disease in clinical practice. *Heart* 2005; **91(Suppl V)**: v1–52.

2 Grundy S. Obesity, metabolic syndrome and coronary atherosclerosis. *Circulation* 2002; **105**: 2696–8.

3 Bloom B. Daily regimen and compliance with treatment. *BMJ* 2001; **323**: 647.

4 Alberti K, Zimmet P, Shaw J. The metabolic syndrome – a new worldwide definition. *Lancet* 2005; **366**: 1059–60.

5 Kahn R, Buse J, Ferrannini E, Stern M. The metabolic syndrome – time for a critical appraisal: joint statement from the American Diabetes Association and the European Association for the Study of Diabetes. *Diabetes Care* 2005; **28**: 2289–304.

6 Wald N, Law M. A strategy to reduce cardiovascular disease by more than 80%. *BMJ* 2003; **326**: 1419.

Abbreviations

ACE	Angiotensin-converting enzyme
ADA	American Diabetes Association
ALLHAT	Antihypertensive and Lipid-Lowering Treatment to Prevent Heart Attack Trial
ALLIANCE	Aggressive Lipid-Lowering Initiation Abates New Cardiac Events
ASCOT	Anglo–Scandinavian Cardiac Outcomes Trial
ATP	Adult Treatment Panel
BHS	British Hypertension Society
BMI	Body mass index
CARDS	Collaborative Atorvastatin Diabetes Study
CB_1	Cannabinoid receptor 1
CHD	Coronary heart disease
CRF	Chronic renal failure
CRP	C-reactive protein
CT	Computed tomography
CVA	Cerebrovascular accident
CVD	Cardiovascular disease
DBP	Diastolic blood pressure
DCCT	Diabetes Control and Complications Trial
DM	Diabetes mellitus
EASD	European Association for the Study of Diabetes
ECG	Electrocardiogram
EGIR	European Group for the Study of Insulin Resistance
EUROASPIRE	European Action on Secondary and Primary Prevention by Intervention to Reduce Events
GMS	General Medical Services
GPwSI	GP with special interest
HbA_{1C}	Glycated haemoglobin
HDL	High density lipoprotein
HDL-C	High density lipoprotein cholesterol
HOPE	Heart Outcomes Prevention Evaluation
HOT	Hypertension Optimal Treatment
HPS	Heart Protection Study
IDF	International Diabetes Federation
IFG	Impaired fasting glucose
IGT	Impaired glucose tolerance
IL	Interleukin
IT	Information technology
JBS	Joint British Societies
LDL	Low density lipoprotein
LDL-C	Low density lipoprotein cholesterol
LIFE	Losartan Intervention For Endpoint Reduction in Hypertension
MI	Myocardial infarction
MRI	Magnetic Resonance Imaging
NCEP	National Cholesterol Education Program
NHANES	National Health and Nutrition Examination Survey
NHS	National Health Service

NICE	National Institute for Health and Clinical Excellence
NNT	Number needed to treat
NSF	National Service Framework
PAI	Plasminogen activator inhibitor
PBC	Practice based commissioning
PbR	Payment by results
PCO	Primary Care Organisation
PCT	Primary Care Trust
PROACTIVE	Prospective Pioglitazone Clinical Trial in Macrovascular Events
PROVE-IT	Pravastatin or Atorvastatin Evaluation and Infection Therapy
QOF	Quality and Outcomes Framework
REVERSAL	Reversal of Atherosclerosis with Aggressive Lipid Lowering
RIO	Rimonabant In Obesity
SBP	Systolic blood pressure
TC	Total cholesterol
TIA	Transient ischaemic attack
TNF	Tumour necrosis factor
TNT	Treating to New Targets
UKPDS	United Kingdom Prospective Diabetes Study
VLDL-C	Very low density lipoprotein cholesterol
WHO	World Health Organization
WHR	Waist-to-hip ratio
WOSCOPS	West of Scotland Coronary Prevention Study